BRANDS
with
CHARACTER

BASHEER
GRAPHIC BOOKS

CHAPTERS

Foreword

We bring you the circus — that Pied Piper whose magic tunes lead children of all ages, from 6 to 60, into a tinseled and spun-candied world of reckless beauty and mounting laughter; whirling thrills; of rhythm, excitement and grace; of daring, enflaring and dance; of high-stepping horses and high-flying stars.

But behind all this, the circus is a massive machine whose very life depends on discipline, motion and speed... a mechanized army on wheels that rolls over any obstacle in its path... that meets calamity again and again, but always comes up smiling... a place where disaster and tragedy stalk the Big Top, haunt the backyards, and ride the circus rails... where Death is constantly watching for one frayed rope, one weak link, or one trace of fear.

A fierce, primitive fighting force that smashes relentlessly forward against impossible odds: That is the circus. And this is the story of the biggest of the Big Tops... and of the men and women who fight to make it — *The Greatest Show on Earth!*

An excerpt from the opening sequence of the 1952 classic, *The Greatest Show on Earth,* directed, produced and narrated by Cecil B. DeMille. It tells the story behind the scenes of the world largest railroad circus, Ringling Bros. and Barnum & Bailey Circus, cramming real life thrills and experiences, and unfolding the lives of these entertainers on either side of the huge circus canvas.

So you might wonder what the circus have got to do with the characters presented in this book? Behind the veil of laughters and the entertaining acts performed by the circus troupe, lies problems that are very real and practical in the world we live in; economic viability, safety hazards, people mismanagement. And despite all the problems, these performers, man and creatures alike, will always present their best and showcase their greatest performance to the audiences.

Much like branding with mascots and characters, behind those cute little monsters or the cape wearing protector of justice, lies a whole team of people that presents the best image possible for a product or service. And in the hands of graphic designers, illustrators and artists alike, we paint, draw, sculpt, sketch and finally, we breathe new life to a character that will be the face of the company in years to come.

Where performers compete for the center ring for a shot at stardom, the usage of mascots and characters is also similarly an attempt to identify power and ownership, where only the strongest survive. Much like our predecessors, early mankind began leaving marks to signify ownership or to identify themselves with political and religious power. The pharaohs of the great Egypt empire left their marks (or brand) in the form of hieroglyphs and the colossal Roman Caesars commissioned artists to create sculptures in their own image. In modern times, this has been translated to commerce and businesses: talking tigers and happy green geckos have been served as persuasive voices and faces for their respective brands, much like the gravity defying flying trapeze or the charming illusionists as the star of the show.

Brands with Character is classified into four chapters, using similes to describe the nature and characteristics of the brand, mascot or character—"Brave as Lion" showcases heroic characters that we often admire or aspire to be; "Playful as Sealion" exhibits the acrobatic, agile and playful characteristics of the characters; "Happy as Clown" compiles the characters that will often make you smile, and remind us that there is a kid in all of us; and "Hungry as Bear" presents the characters that will make your stomach growl!

Brands with Character compiles a collection of mascots and character who have been performing well for their brands, much like the animals and stars of the circus. And sometime in the future, we'll grow old with them, remembering how we used to love them, much like how we remembered and awed at the performances of the circus. And like how *The Greatest Show on Earth* ends, "The show must go on."

As playful as
SEALION

Red Bear Survival Camp

–

Studio   Bunpei Ginza

Design   Bunpei Yorifuji, Ayaka Kitatani

–

Based on the main theme of a workshop involving the use of fire, the character was created by combining the visual elements of a fire—the main theme of the camp—as well as, a bear and a tent to represent the idea of a workshop. The bear character was expanded and used on various items like the tents and gloves.

Yeah! Burger

–

Studio	Tad Carpenter Creative
Design	Tad Carpenter

–

Yeah! Burger is a modern burger dining concept based on sourcing local food and making healthy diet choices. It prides itself on offering local meats, grains and food produced in Atlanta-Georgia area. The extensive use of happy and bright colours in its visual identity has been applied onto quirky badges, through to the menu, T-shirts and other collateral.

ERIK MAIER
MANAGING PARTNER
erik@yeahburger.com

1168 Howell Mill Road | Suite E | Atlanta, Georgia | 30318
P 404.496.4393 | F 404.496.4968 | M 404.386.3561
facebook.com/yeahburger | twitter.com/yeahburger

YEAHBURGER.COM

YEAH! BURGER

BURGERS & MORE

All of our patties are made with organic or natural ingredients and are free of antibiotic, hormones and preservatives. All of our meats are humanely-raised. Our burgers and sandwiches are always cooked fresh, right when you order!

① CHOOSE YOUR PATTY

BEEF BURGER	BISON BURGER	TURKEY BURGER	VEGGIE BURGER	GRILLED CHICKEN BREAST SANDWICH
A double stack of grass-fed, Georgia-raised beef	Colorado grass-fed bison	Certified organic turkey	Made with certified organic Sea Island red peas	Certified organic chicken
$6.99	$7.99	$5.99	$5.99	$5.99

② CHOOSE YOUR BUN

SOUTHERN WHITE	WHOLE WHEAT	GLUTEN-FREE WHITE	LETTUCE WRAP
Made with organic flour by H&F bakery	Made with organic flour by H&F bakery	Add $1.25	Green leaf lettuce

③ TOP IT OFF!

ADD CHEESE!
Certified organic cheeses
$1 EACH
AMERICAN   PEPPER JACK
BLUE   PIMENTO
CHEDDAR   SWISS

FREE TOPPINGS
Go for it!
LETTUCE   CHOPPED VIDALIA ONIONS *Organic*
TOMATO   SLICED VIDALIA ONIONS *Organic*
DILL PICKLES   GRILLED VIDALIA ONIONS *Organic*
JALAPENOS   SUNFLOWER SPROUTS

PREMIUM TOPPINGS
$1 EACH
NITRATE-FREE BACON   SLICED AVOCADO
TURKEY BACON   SHAUN'S RED CHILI
SAUTÉED MUSHROOMS   NAPA COLESLAW
CAGE-FREE FRIED EGG *Organic*

④ GET SAUCED!

All sauces are FREE on your burger or sandwich! Try as a dipping sauce with fries for $.50 EACH.

YEAH! SAUCE	ROASTED GARLIC AIOLI	MISSISSIPPI HOP BBQ
KETCHUP	HONEY MUSTARD	WHITE BBQ
MUSTARD	DUKE'S MAYO	ROOSTER SAUCE
	BACON JAM	
	HOT ALABAMA RELISH	
	BLACK PEPPERCORN STEAK	

HOT DOGS

Featuring Let's be Frank all-natural hot dogs! Served on a Southern White bun made with organic flour

THE CLASSIC	$4.99
Grass-fed beef hot dog with your choice of toppings from above	
SOUTHERN DOG	$5.99
Grass-fed beef hot dog topped with Pimento cheese, chopped Vidalia onions and hot Alabama relish	
CHILI & CHEESE DOG	$5.99
Grass-fed beef hot dog topped with Shaun's red chili, organic American cheese and jalapenos	

SALADS

All of our salads are made with organic lettuce!

SIMPLE GREENS	$5.99
Lettuce, cucumber, radish and fresh herb lemon vinaigrette	
WITH GRILLED ORGANIC CHICKEN $9.99	
CAESAR SALAD	$5.99
Lettuce, croutons, Parmigiano cheese and Caesar dressing	
WITH GRILLED ORGANIC CHICKEN $9.99	
CLASSIC COBB	$9.99
Lettuce, avocado, nitrate-free bacon, grilled organic chicken, hardboiled egg, organic blue cheese crumbles and Johnston Family Farms buttermilk ranch dressing	

SIDES $2.49 EACH
Add dipping sauce for $.50!

We use 100% heart-healthy canola oil for our fries, onion rings and pickles!

HAND-CUT FRENCH FRIES	FRIED PICKLES
GLUTEN-FREE FRENCH FRIES	KETTLE POTATO CHIPS $1.49
BUTTERMILK VIDALIA ONION RINGS	CUP OF SHAUN'S RED CHILI
FIFTY-FIFTY	CUP OF NAPA COLESLAW
Half French fries, half onion rings	

KIDDIE COMBOS

All Kiddie Combos come with french fries, choice of an organic milk box or organic apple juice

BURGER COMBO	$6.99
Single patty grass-fed beef burger	
HOT DOG COMBO	$6.99
Grass-fed beef hot dog	

ALL ITEMS LISTED AS ORGANIC ARE USDA CERTIFIED ORGANIC. HERE'S TO KEEPING FOOD REAL!
PRINTED ON RECYCLED PAPER. © 2010 YEAH! BURGER. ALL RIGHTS RESERVED.

🍦 ICE CREAM
Featuring Strauss Family Creamery organic soft-serve ice cream!

MILK SHAKES
Made with certified organic milk!
$4.99 EACH
CHOCOLATE
VANILLA
STRAWBERRY
PEACH
COFFEE
COOKIES AND CREAM
WHYNATTE

FLOATS
Featuring Boylan sodas with 100% cane sugar
$4.99 EACH
BROWN COW
Vanilla ice cream with Root Beer
BLACK COW
Vanilla ice cream with Black Cherry soda
CREAMSICLE
Vanilla ice cream with Orange soda

CONCRETES $4.99 EACH
Vanilla soft-serve ice cream blended at high speed with your favorite mix-ins!
Your first mix-in is free! Add more for $.50 EACH.

MIX-INS
HOT FUDGE   CHOPPED PEANUTS   CHOCOLATE ALMOND BARK
COOKIES AND CREAM   PEANUT BRITTLE   CHOCOLATE ESPRESSO BEANS
PEANUT BUTTER CUPS   HEATH CANDY BAR

SUNDAES $4.99 EACH
Your choice of CHOCOLATE or VANILLA soft-serve ice cream in a cup with HOT FUDGE,
CHOPPED PEANUTS and FRESH WHIPPED CREAM

CUPS $2.99 EACH
Your choice of CHOCOLATE or VANILLA soft-serve ice cream

🍾 BEVERAGES
Alcoholic

BEER

DRAFTS	GLASS	PITCHER
BROWN LAGER Brooklyn Brewery	$5	$18
DOPPELBOCK Spaten Optimator	$5	$18
INDIA PALE ALE Harpoon	$5	$18
PALE ALE Sweetwater 420	$5	$18
TRIPEL ALE Chimay White	$8	$30

BOTTLES & CANS
INDIA PALE ALE Bison IPA *Organic* $5
LAGER Pabst Blue Ribbon $3
LAGER Budweiser $3
LIGHT LAGER Bud Light $3
LIGHT LAGER Amstel Light $5
PALE LAGER Stella Artois $5
GLUTEN-FREE Green's Amber Ale $8

WINE

RED WINES
CABERNET SAUVIGNON Leese-Fitch, Sonoma '08 $8
MALBEC Yellow+Blue, Argentina '08 *Organic* $6
PINOT NOIR Wild Hog, Russian River Valley '08 $8
SYRAH Qupé, Central California Coast '07 $12

WHITE WINES
CHARDONNAY Estancia, Monterey County '08 $8
PINOT GRIGIO Cana Defra, Italy '08 $8
ROSÉ Domaine de Nizas, France '08 $6
SAUVIGNON BLANC Yellow+Blue, Chile '08 *Organic* $6

SPIRITS

GIN
GORDON'S $7
BEEFEATER $8

RUM
CAPTAIN MORGAN $7
CRUZAN $7
HORNÉ SPICED RUM $7
GOSLING'S BLACK RUM $8

TEQUILA
CONQUISTADOR $7
PATRON SILVER $10

VODKA
PRAIRIE ORGANIC $7
GREY GOOSE $9
BELVEDERE $10

WHISKIES
OLD OVERHOLT $6
EVAN WILLIAMS $6
FOUR ROSES SM. BATCH $7
JACK DANIEL'S $8
JAMESON $8
JOHNNIE WALKER RED $8
RUSSELL'S RESERVE RYE $8
BASIL HAYDEN'S $8
MAKER'S MARK $9
HIGH WEST SILVER $10
HIGH WEST RENDEZVOUS $10
WOODFORD RESERVE $10

SIGNATURE COCKTAILS

MARGARITA Conquistador tequila, triple sec, lime and Hawaiian sea salt $8
MOJITO Cruzan rum, mortified mint and lime $8
FROZEN STRAWBERRY DAIQUIRI Rum, strawberries, lemon and ice $8
RUBY RED EYE Absolut Ruby Red vodka, Campari and fresh grapefruit juice $9
CRITICAL MASS Tuaca liqueur, Chimay White beer and fresh orange juice $9
COMSTOCK MULE High West Silver whiskey, ginger beer and lime $9
DARK & STORMY Gosling's Black Rum, ginger beer and lime $9
FATHER'S OFFICE Johnnie Walker Red whiskey, Cherry Heering, fresh orange juice $9
RYE TOAST Old Overholt Rye whiskey, Cynar liqueur and lemon bitters $8
MANHATTAN Russell's Reserve Rye, sweet vermouth and bitters $8

PRINTED ON RECYCLED PAPER. © 2010 YEAH! BURGER. ALL RIGHTS RESERVED.

🥤 BEVERAGES
Non-Alcoholic

SODA

DRAFTS $1.75
Featuring Coca-Cola products
COKE
DIET COKE
COKE ZERO
SPRITE
MELLOW YELLOW
DR. PEPPER
BARQ'S ROOT BEER

BOTTLES $2
Boylan sodas made with 100% cane sugar
ROOT BEER
ORANGE
CREAM
BLACK CHERRY

TEA

BREWED $1.75
Revolution Tea iced teas
SWEET TEA
UNSWEETENED TEA

BOTTLED $2
GREEN TEA *Organic*

OTHER DRINKS

JUICES
ORANGE JUICE Fresh-squeezed $3
GRAPEFRUIT JUICE Fresh-squeezed $3
ORGANIC APPLE JUICE POUCH $2

SPARKLING BEVERAGES $2
IZZE Clementine
IZZE Peach

ENERGY DRINKS
RED BULL $2.50
RED BULL SUGAR-FREE $2.50
WHYNATTE $2.25

VITAMIN WATER $2
LEMONADE Multi-V
ORANGE Essential
TROPICAL CITRUS Energy

WATER
FILTERED WATER   FREE
BOTTLED WATER FIJI $1.75
SPARKLING WATER San Pellegrino $2

MILK $2
Horizon organic milk boxes
CHOCOLATE
STRAWBERRY
WHITE

1168 Howell Mill Road | Suite E
Atlanta, Georgia | 30318
P 404.496.4393 | F 404.496.4368
facebook.com/yeahburger | twitter.com/yeahburger

YEAHBURGER.COM

Eventyrbrus

—

Design   Mikael Fløysand, Julie Elise Hauge
Photography   Mikael Fløysand

—

Mikael Fløysand and Julie Elise Hauge designed
a new packaging for the Norwegian soda,
Eventyrbrus, which was inspired by the clever fox
character from traditional Norwegian fairy tales.
The concept behind the packaging is that of a
little prankster with a fun and playful image.

Aki Happy Smile

—

Design   Akinori Oishi

—

Akinori Oishi is best know for the symbolic "Aki Happy Smile" character. It is easily recognizable and its simplicity allows it to be developed into various media, art & design, animation and interactive applications. Aki Happy Smile's cheerful universe can help communicate to its audience in a friendly manner for projects around the world.

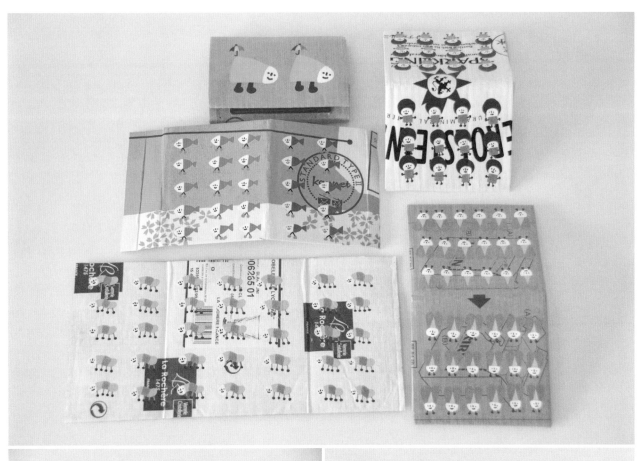

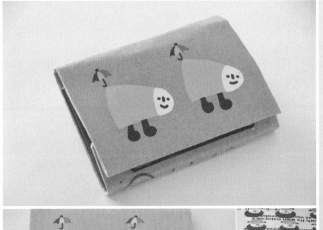

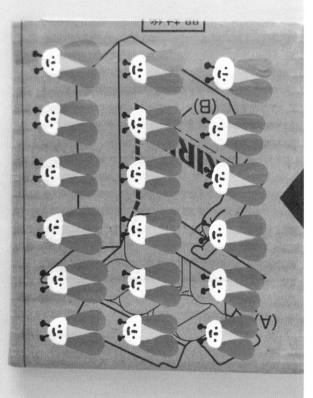

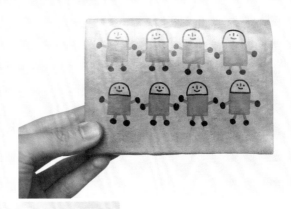

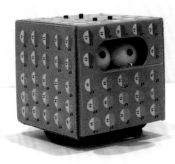

BEAMS

–

Studio	Neandertal
Creative Direction	Takuma Takasaki
Art Direction	Gen Ishii
Design	Tokiko Fujioji
Illustration	100%Orange

–

A seasonal campaign for BEAMS, a fashion and lifestyle emporium with roots in Harajuku, Tokyo, during the Autumn/Winter campaign. Under the theme of "Let's fall in love", portraits of real lovers for the Spring/Summer campaign by photographer Kotori Kawashima, were illustrated by 100%Orange and featured for the Autumn/Winter.

Memit

—

Studio   Hello Monday

—

Memit is a brand new online content storage service
aimed at helping professionals organize, store, and
share knowledge content. To help differentiate Memit
from similar services, Hello Monday formed a visual
identity based on the idea of a squirrel collecting
and storing nuts to create a memorable character
logo to help users understand the service.

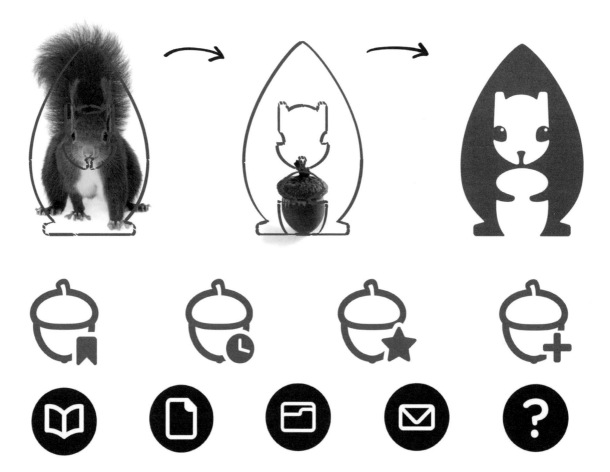

MUJI

–

Studio	Bunpei Ginza
Design	Bunpei Yorifuji, Ayaka Kitatani

–

The round-face character was designed based on the concept of always being prepared for a disaster. The character explains the use and know-how of emergency supplies and disaster prevention items.

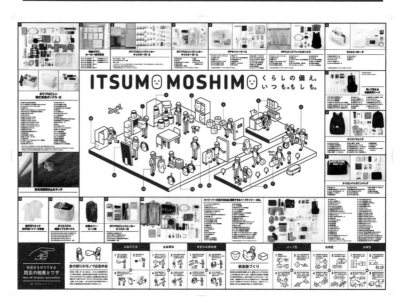

くらしの備え。
いつものもしも。

Home

Office&School

Carry

Children

Storage Space

Rolling Stock "Food"

Rolling Stock "Clothes"

Rolling Stock "Daily Necessities"

Rolling Stock "Preserved Food"

Keep Fit

Comfortable Clothing

Maintenance

Favorite Clothes

Long Trip

Short Trip

ITSUMO MOSHIMO

無印良品

東日本大震災を境に、くらしに対する私たちの意識は大きく変わりました。節電や節水、自然の恵みの活用、先人の気づき…多くの人が、くらしを見直し、生活の基本を取り戻そうとしています。それはそのまま、「もしも」の時の備えにも通じること。どんなに立派な道具や知識でもいざという時に使いこなせなければ本当の備えにはならないということを、私たちは身をもって体験しました。無印良品は、日常のさまざまな「もしも」を想定しながら、身の回りの日用品の中から、「何をどのように備えるか」を提案していきます。日常的に使えて、万一の備えにもなる日用品を上手に使いこなしながら、日々のくらしを快適にしなるもの。そんな日用品を上手に使いこなしていくことで「本当の備え、防災力」となっていくでしょう。

無印良品

Yigloo

–

Studio	Foreign Policy Design Group
Brand Direction	Arthur Chin
Creative Direction	Yah Leng Yu
Art Direction	Yah-Leng Yu
Design	Cheryl Chong, Yah-Leng Yu
Illustration	Cheryl Chong
Space Design	Weiling Lim, Minmin Choo from [+0]

–

Yigloo serves yogurt and revolves around ideas of fun and happiness appealing to both children and adults. Whimsical and quirky characters were specially created and placed at unexpected corners in the store for customers to chance upon. These colourful characters, in contrast to an all-white interior, interact with the real environment. Refurbished and recycled furniture were white washed and reused in the space, indicative of the joint's effort to be eco-friendly.

MOMO

YOGGIE

BONG

TYLER

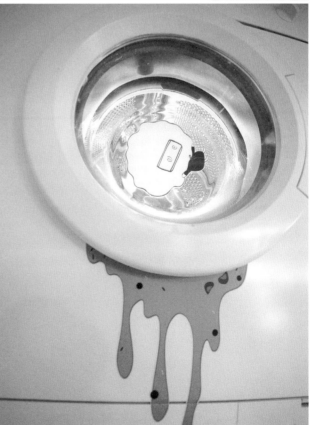

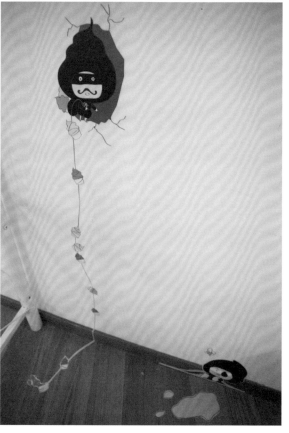

LET'S DO THE
YIGLOO

1 PICK
A CUP

2 MIX
ANY FLAVOR

3 DRESS
ME UP

4 ENJOY
YUM!

Kids Cafe Piccolo

–

Interiors	PODIUM
Graphic	VONSUNG
Photography	(Interior) Budullee Lee for PODIUM, (Graphics) Yu-Kuang

–

The space of Kids Cafe Piccolo was designed and constructed by Design PODIUM in Seoul for children and their parents, consisting of a playground, playroom, party room, library and cafe. The identity of the café was created using Roman letters instead of Korean letters to make learning more enjoyable and interactive.

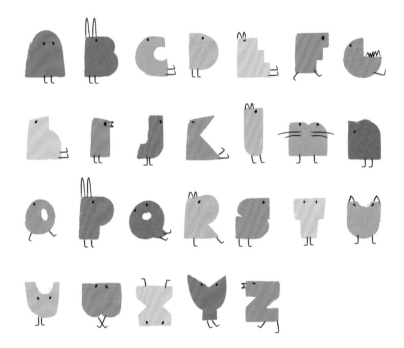

KIDS
CAFE 피콜로
PICCOLO

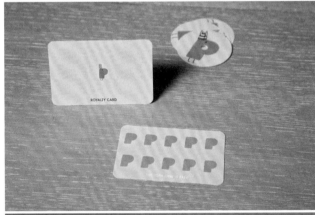

CHI-BA+KUN

–

Design   Chiharu Sakazaki

–

CHI-BA+KUN is creature living in Chiba prefecture, Japan that loves a challenge and is full of curiosity. The side profile of CHI-BA+KUN resembles the geographical boundaries of the Chiba prefecture. The character was first created as a mascot in 2007 as a mascot for the national sport festival held in the Chiba prefecture three years later. Due to its popularity during the event, CHI-BA+KUN was adopted as the official mascot of Chiba prefecture since 2011.

Dreambox

–

Creative Direction	Dreambox
Art Direction	Pigologist
Illustrations	Pigologist
Photography	Dreambox, Istanbul

–

The illustrations are a reflection of Dreambox's story, branding and what they do, created in the colours of their brand. They are installed on the entrance, glass doors and glass walls of Dreambox's office.

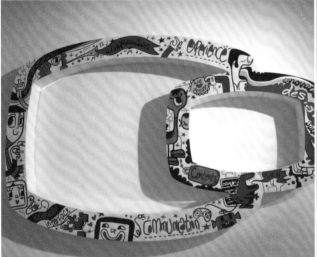

Nuts for Snack

–

Studio   mousegraphics

–

Nuts can be a lot of fun and also have high
nutritional value especially when oven-baked as
in this case. We decided to opt for a consumer-
friendly, casual looking yet careful approach, to
combine both attributes in the best possible way.

We developed the "Nuts for Snack" product
name which plays on the double meaning of the
word "nuts"; to "go crazy" over a type of food
so as to make it a daily small nibble ritual.

We worked on the packaging design with an emphasis
on illustration collaborated with someone who has
worked with urban graffiti and fanzine illustration. It
lead us to decide on several cartoon-like characters.

Both cute and awkward, in funky, nut-related
color schemes, these characters are assigned
to the different product flavors and ultimately
'communicate' in a globally recognized urban jargon.

PlusPlus

–

Studio	Build
Character	Edik Katykhin
Typeface	Si Billam
Animation	Animade
Sound	Sonica Studio

–

Build were commissioned by Ukrainian TV channel 1+1 to create the brand identity for their new children's channel, PlusPlus. The identity was based on a series of illustrations of a family—mum, dad and child— which were designed to create a fully flexible and dynamic branding system, with varying colours, shapes and expressions. The characters were used in all on-air and off-air promotion, as well as a series of teasers and indents. As well as the characters, Build also produced a customised typeface, on-air menu systems and comprehensive brand guidelines.

Osaka Shoin Women's College

–

Studio　Canaria
Design　Yuji Tokuda

–

With the setup of a new department specialising in multimedia characters and literature in 2009, a character was created by designing a face that contains the abbreviations of the department's name. The concept of the advertisements is based on the idea of training people who "grows" characters. The core media used in the campaign is through the mobile phones, with the character "growing" up with constant communication. Users can also receive college information through the character or get a mail of encouragement during entrance examinations.

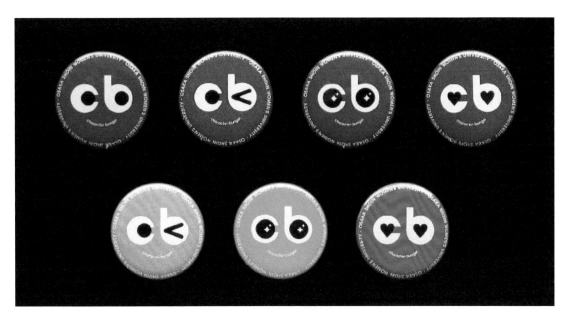

Tohato Caramel Corn

—

Art direction   Sugiyama Yuki
Design   Hitomi Kojima, Wakana Saito

—

Caramel Corn is a snack food that is hugely popular for over 40 years in Japan. With the redesign of its packaging, over 150 kinds of special characters are designed according to seasonal events such as Santa Claus during Christmas and dolls during the Doll Festival (Japanese traditional event for girls), in addition to classic red packaging. Special flavours that are created over the years, also have characters designed for the respective flavours.

 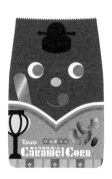 

Paz Holandesa Hospital

–

Design   Rejane Dal Bello

–

Paz Holandesa Hospital is a non-profit children's hospital in Arequipa, Peru. Together with Yomar Augusto, Rejane Dal Bello sponsored the identity for this hospital. It is a great working process with the creator of the hospital (Marjan van Mourik) who is devoted to this amazing project and is inspirational for the development of the design. Initiated in 2005, the ongoing visual identity includes logo, stationery, folders, cards and signages, wall paintings, games, editorial.

Paz Holandesa

Urb. Villa Continetal Calle 4
nr.101 Paucarpata
Arequipa Peru
t +51 0 54432281
e info@pazholandesa.com

Paz Holandesa
Urb Villa Continetal
Calle 4 nr 101
Paucarpata Arequipa Peru
t +51 0 54432281

ROSEMARY SILVA
Ouvidoria IAMSPE
0800 7708 144

Buena Salud

Buena Salud

Buena Salud

Buena Salud

Baño de Hombres

Baño de Mujeres

baño privado

extinguidores

teléfono público

sistema contra incendios

doutora

doutor

inscription

zona segura en caso de sismo

rampa para discapacitados

salida

Akaihane Kyodo Bokin

–

Studio	machine inc.
Design	Emi Tomita, Chiharu Sakazaki

–

Special Tosho card/Quo card (prepaid cards) are
available for purchase as donations for Akaihane
Kyodo Bokin. Responding to the request from
donors to have something practical in return
for their donation instead of a red feather, the
prepaid card was first introduced in the late
1980s. The characters designed by Chiharu
Sakazaki have been featured since 2009.

Bijutsu Shuppan Service Center

–

Design	Chiharu Sakazaki
Photography	Rintaroh Abe

–

Bijutsu Shuppan Service Center co., ltd. delivers art learning program service (planning/sales) for school education. Chiharu Sakazaki, who was very popular among young women, was asked to design the character to target the increasing amount of young female teachers. Based on the client's request for a charming and friendly character, "Tube-kun" was created. "Tube-kun" has contributed to the higher recognition of the company through its appearance in the items that teachers often see, such as printed matters, products, public relations and packaging.

Joyful Kindergarten

–

Studio   gardens&co.

–

Joyful is one of the newest international nursery & kindergarten. They are committed to providing a vibrant and enriching learning environment where kids can feel joyful and safe. After three months of intensive developments, gardens&co. created everything from scratch, applying the "smile" shape from the logo throughout the entire branding communication, from uniforms to wall graphics to stuffed animals.

joyful

English International Kindergarten & Nursery

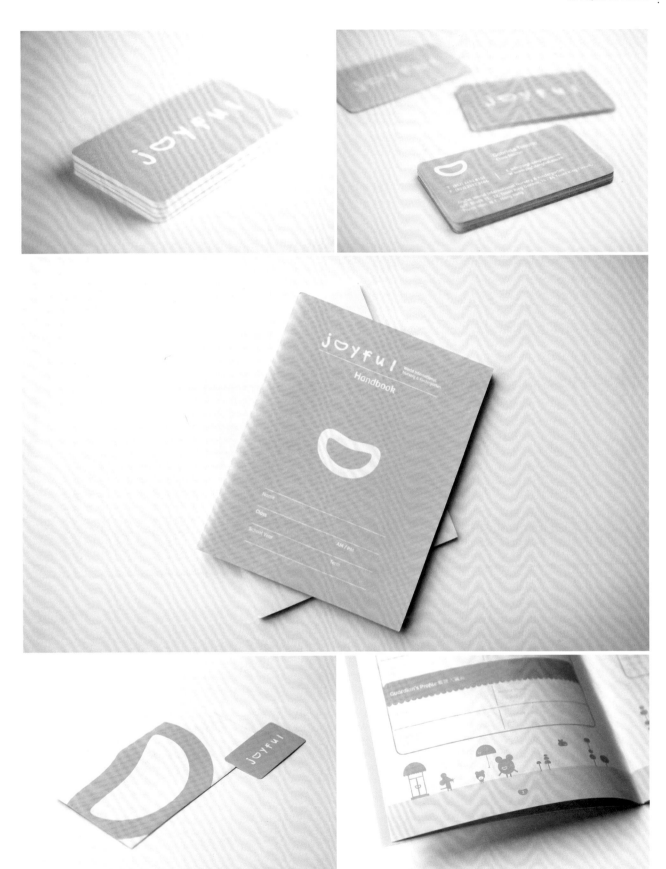

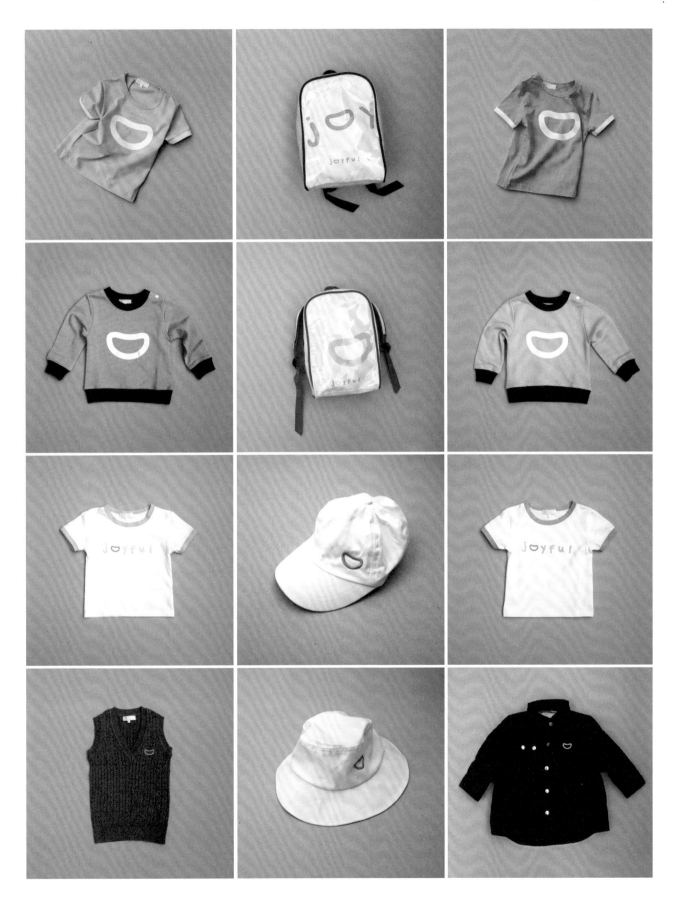

Gubble Bum

–

Studio	JJAAKK
Design	Jesse Kirsch

–

Jesse Kirsch designs the packaging for a
fun and slightly twisted bubble gum brand.
Beneath the cutesy, colourful exterior lies an
unexpected twist when you remove the outer
box—revealing the skeleton of each gubble bum.

Cheeky Monkey

—

Studio   Jamfactory

—

Cheeky Monkey's Fun House is a club house specially operated for kids below the age of 12, providing different kinds of playgroups, English and phonics classes, sports and activities, parties, etc. These activities are conducted by professional instructors. With the first and largest indoor three storeys play frame in Hong Kong, kids are guaranteed to have a fun and special time, and parents are guaranteed that their kids can play and learn in a safe and hygienic place.

A sister company with Cheeky Monkey's Fun House, Cheeky Monkey's English focuses on providing English education and life coaching of kids from the age of 3–12.

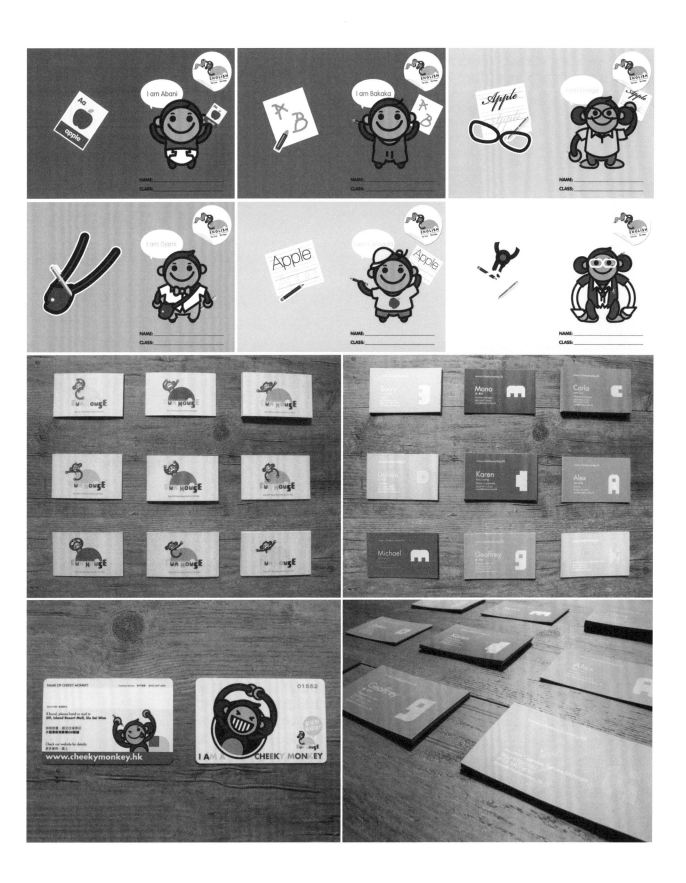

Columbia

–

Design   Tarout
Client   Columbia Sports

–

Tarout designed the character for the footwear "Forest
Park: tarout edition" by Columbia Sports in 2011.
The footwear was made for women who like nature.
Columbie, the character, is printed on its foot bed,
as well as on the leather charms as a small gift.

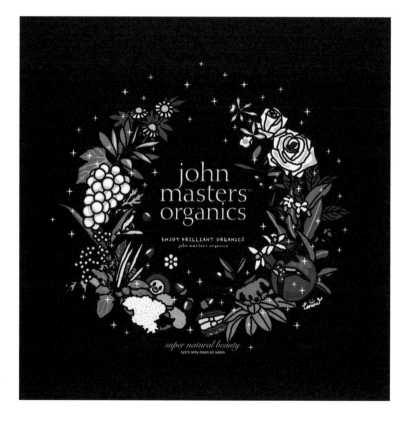

Aminals

–

Studio	Design Positive
Design	Scott Lambert
Photography	Rama Salem

–

Aminals, a family focused centre in Bahrain, was conceived to understand the needs of parents whilst never forgetting what it is like to be a child. Aminals offers learning classes, relaxation, and refreshments for all, and most importantly it is a place for kids to go wild. The strategy was built around pillars of fun, empathy, empowerment, and trust. The playful identity and name sidestep all the cliches of the genre.

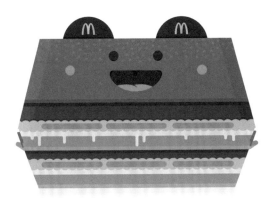

McCute

–

Design   Joao Ricardo Machado

–

Joao Ricardo Machado was invited by Bill Tikos, from thecoolhunter.com, to design a limited edition packaging for a McDonald's new thematic mobile space—the McDonald's Fun Cart. The idea was to create something very friendly and cute, just like the space would be. The original shape of the packages was maintained, but each package was turned into a character with a smiling face.

Milkraft

–

Creative Direction	Hirotoshi Fukuda
Art Direction	Miyako Kodama, Ryo Ueda
Design	Miyako Kodama, Ryo Ueda, Minami Mabuchi
Copywriting	Kosuke Ikehata
Photography	Sukehiro Nakamura
Production	COMMUNE, Futaba
Producer	Atsuhiro Kondo
Project Management	Hirotoshi Fukuda
Planning	Hirotoshi Fukuda, Kosuke Ikehata, Miyako Kodama, Ryo Ueda
Programming	Tomoko Yamazaki
Assistant	Yukiko Hayashi

–

Commune was asked to design the brand for Milkraft, a company that deals with paper and packaging. As Milkraft uses recycled paper from milk cartons, the logo is designed to reflect the cartons and printed on a rustic texture to resemble the cartons.

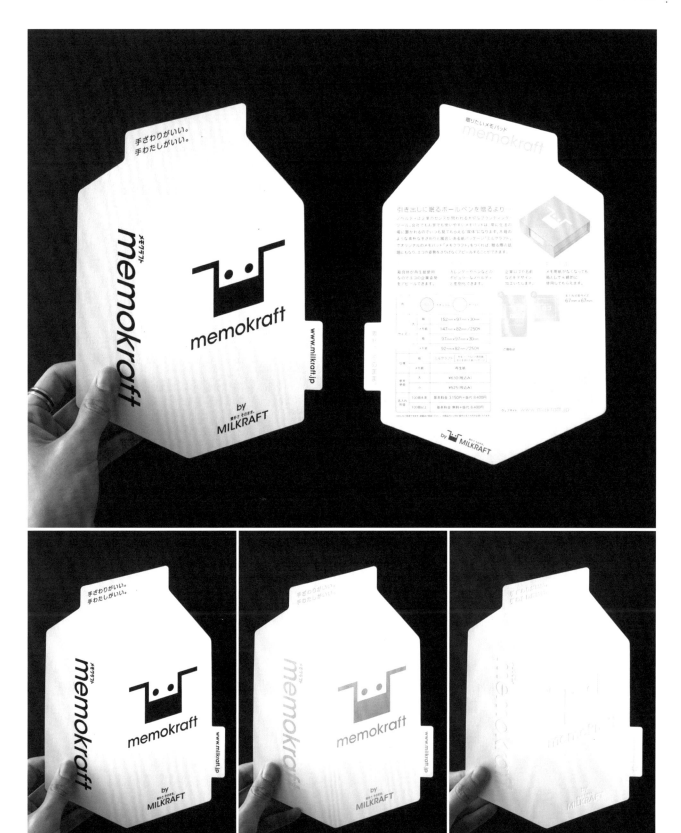

Oh! Mai Mai!

–

Design   Jorge Artola
Web Development   John Del Valle

–

Oh! Mai Mai!® its a dangerous and cute typeface created by Jorge Artola. Inspired by the mai mai monster® it is fully equipped with numerals, accents, punctuation, special characters, and also includes a bonus wallpaper pack.

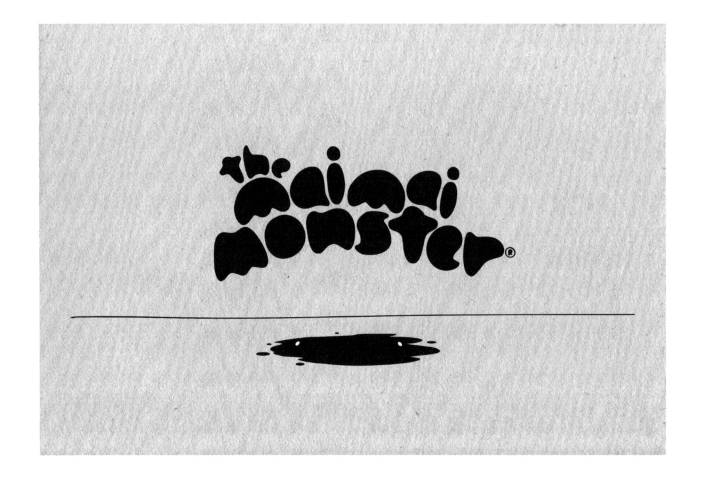

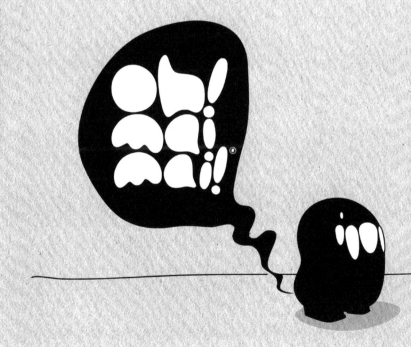

Oh! Mai Mai!
REGULAR OPEN TYPE
BASIC CHARACTERS

ABCDEFGHIJKLM
NOPQRSTUVWXYZ
abcdefghijklm
nopqrstuvwxyz
1234567890

NK Departmental Store

–

Design Sac Magique
Collaboration Lowe Brindfors

–

Sac Magique designed these characters for the NK
department store in Stockholm. These were used
on the packaging for the children's department.

Design Wars

–

Studio   Noeeko
Design   Michal Sycz

–

Design Wars is a brand new platform for people
to submit and buy T-shirt designs created by
artists from around the world. Designers upload
their T-shirt designs to the website, where visitors
and members of the community rate them.
Winning designs are then selected for printing,
with the designers receiving a cash price.

nepia

–

Studio	DESIGN BASE, Dentsu
Design	Tamio Abe, Hiroshi Deshimaru

–

Mr. Hand-san was created for the promotion
campaign of nepia's slim-shaped box tissue.
The character was designed to be a hand
to emphasize its compact handy size.

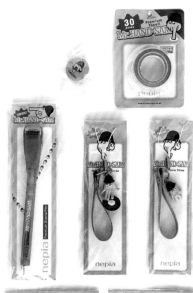

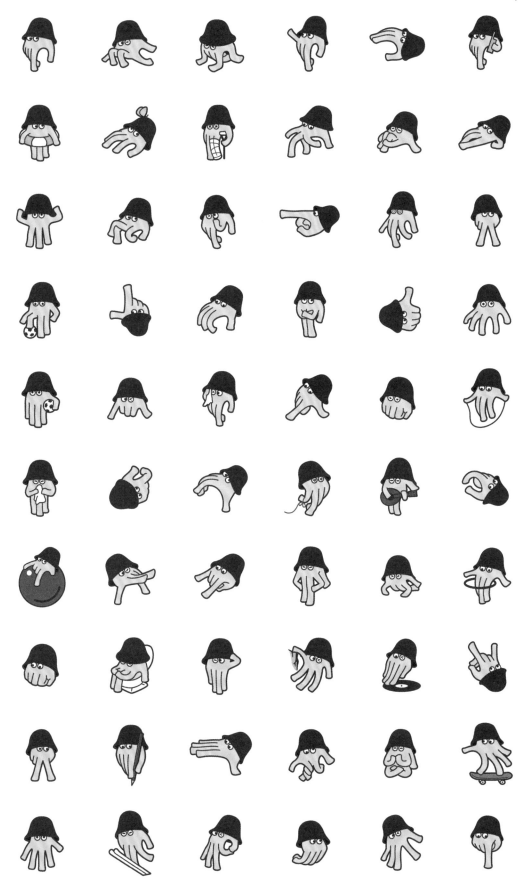

Will & Jamie's

–

Studio   Designers Anonymous
Design   Christian Eager, Darren Barber

–

Will & Jamie's is a brand of fresh yoghurt drinks made by two dairy farmers Will Pritchard and Jamie Adams in Pembrokeshire, Wales. Our design solution for the logo/identity was a pantomime cow to establish the nature of their product and Will & Jamie's partnership. The cow is drawn in various positions, to describe a variety of brand messages. For example, when the brand is on the refrigerated truck, the cow is shivering.

Smile Eco

–

Design   Chiharu Sakazaki

–

For "Benesse Life Smile" (http://shop.benesse.
ne.jp/) which is the life style brand by Benesse
Corporation, Chiharu Sakazaki created the white
bear character as the symbol of their "Eco"
project and products based on their request.

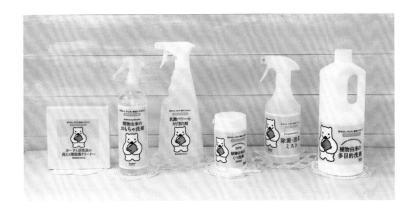

Mr Bean

–

Studio	Ukulele Brand Consultants
Design	Lynn Lim, Yohji Neoh

–

One of Singapore's most recognisable brand mascots, this now-iconic Mr Bean is also an iconoclast. Conceived by Ukulele Brand Consultants at a time when branding—not to mention character branding—was highly unusual for local food & beverage brands, this cuddly, adorable bean personifies the brand's overarching philosophy of "Life's Simple Pleasures". In fact, so universal is the appeal that it catapulted Mr Bean from one humble kiosk to a leading food & beverage chain with over 60 outlets islandwide, with overseas presence in Japan, China and the Philippines.

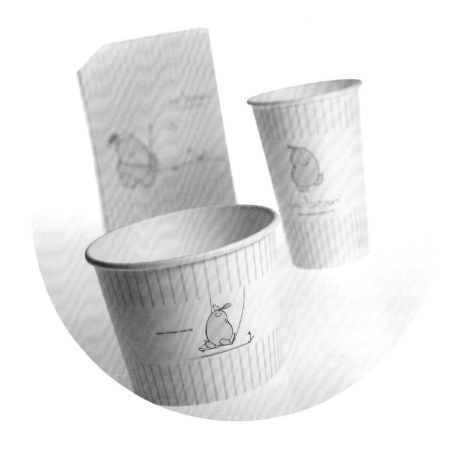

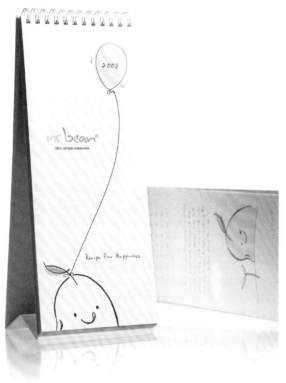

Momiji

–

Studio	Studio Pounce
Photography	Studio Pounce
Client	Momiji

–

Momiji are small collectable dolls which can hold secret written messages inside them. In 2009, Momiji began working with Studio Pounce after connecting through a Momiji Doll Design Competition. The doll packaging was Momiji's first project, and Studio Pounce was asked to create graphics for nine doll boxes in the shape of takeaway noodle boxes. The challenge was to turn the three-dimensional dolls into two-dimensional mascots, these mascots will then be the primary selling point, as well as being featured on the packaging. From then on, Studio Pounce and Momiji have produced many Momiji products together including graphics for textiles, stickers, mugs, notebooks, pens, pocket mirrors and catalogue designs. In 2010, Momiji commissioned Studio Pounce to design three Christmas dolls to be sold globally for a limited time over the festive season.

Fields "P45"

–

Studio	DESIGN BASE, butterfly · stroke inc.
Design	Tamio Abe

–

The project for the growth in new fans of pachinko (pinball machine). The character of "P" describes the project with fun.

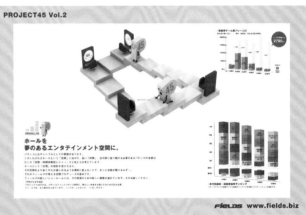

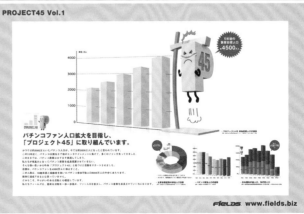

Herokid

—

Design   Andreu Zaragoza

—

Herokid™ is a clothing brand created by Robert Roman (Registred Kid), drawing references from the culture of skateboarding and street art on the streets of Barcelona. The concept for this package was to create a box that can be used a T-shirt package as well as for decorative and promotional collaterals. The Herokid™ logo served as an inspiration for the design of the corrugated carton packaging that needs no adhesive for assembling.

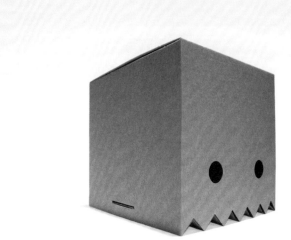

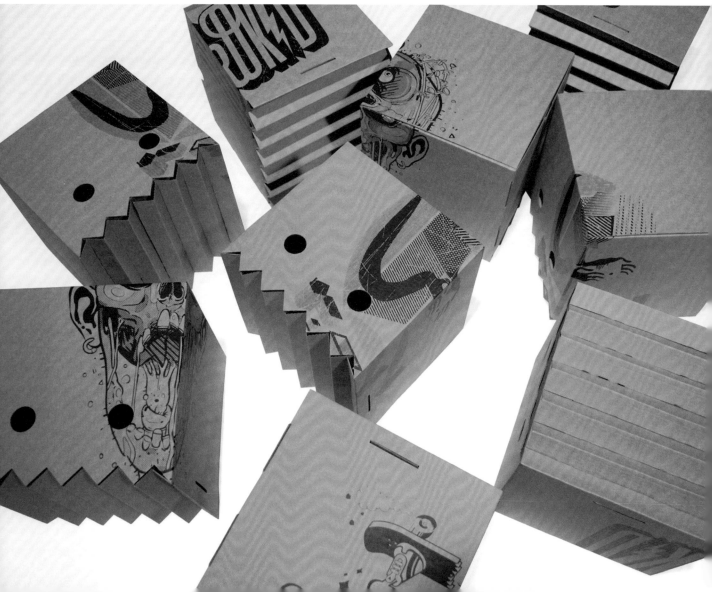

Nyastera

–

Studio	MUZIKA
Design	Mizuki Totori

–

Nyastera, won the judges' approval in 2009 for the Nagasaki National Athletic Meet 2014 Mascot Design Competition. The character was based on two keywords, "Castella" and "Omagari Neko" (尾曲がり猫), that best represent the natural surrounds and daily lives of people living in Nagasaki. Castella is a delicious cake and a famous specialty in Nagasaki, whereas the Omagari Neko is a special breed of cat with a curved tail and is commonly found in Nagasaki. When these two words combine, it forms a character which brings forward the gentleness of the citizens of Nagasaki, and also its friendly image from a global perspective. To put forward the notion of cheerfulness of the Omagari Neko, the onomatopoeic word, "nya-a-a", is used to represent the sound of a cat's meow. Combining it with the excellent taste of the Castella cake (Kastera in Japanese), the name "Nyastera" was created for the character.

Kinpachi Mikan

–

Studio	Doppo
Design	Koichi Sugiyama, Yuta Naruse

–

Kinpachi Mikan's oranges have very thin and sweet skins that is so easy to eat even for babies. Based on this concept, the logo mark was designed to look like an orange, and at the same time resembling a baby with a pacifier when the logo is flipped. In addition, the packaging was designed to be reused as a toy box for children.

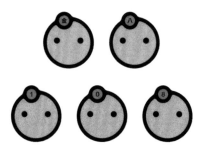

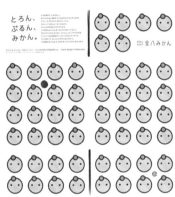

Tower Records

–

Studio	Neandertal
Creative Direction	Takuma Takasaki
Art Direction	Gen Ishii
Illustration	Shigeru Mizuki

–

A publicity campaign for Tower Records' summer sale, Medama Oyaji or "Eyeball Father" is a character from the Japanese horror manga, GeGeGe no Kitaro, and served as a pop kitsch sales promoter at the Tower Records store.

Cuatro Gatos Negros Flacos

–

Design	Laura Varsky
Illustration	Christian Montenegro
Text	Didi Grau

–

"Cuatro gatos negros flacos" or "Four skinny black cats" is a book that plays with four words that repeat, reflect and multiply themselves, words that increase and decrease, horizontal, vertical, diagonal and zigzagging words, with four cats that smile, tease, wink, sleep and stretch themselves.

CUA TRO

GA TOS

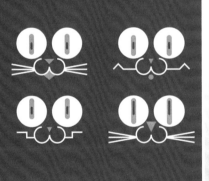

NEG ROS

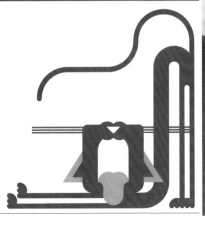

FLA COS

Opuro

–

Studio	Doppo
Design	Koichi Sugiyama, Yuta Naruse

–

Opuro—a bath salt made by a water filter maker—
is soft, gentle and was created to be loved by
people who are concerned with their skin, including
babies and those with sensitive and dry skins. The
character with a visual of a hot spring on its head
(representing public baths in Japan), and the branding
was designed to be simple and symbolic, standing
out amongst the colourful product lineups in stores.

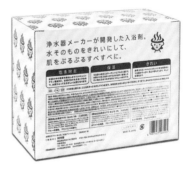

ATARIMAE Project

—

Studio	OZ inc.
Design	Bumpei Yamagata

—

The ATARIMAE Project aims for the improvement of
working environment for people with disabilities, where
they can work "naturally" (or "atarimae" in Japanese)
without any biases or indifference in the society. In
its website, the charming A-shape characters in blue
and orange appear on the messaging system called
ATARIMAE SENGEN (or "declaration of Atarimae"
in Japanese), to represent each posted message.

Kragujevac

—

Studio	Dizajn Studio Box
Creative Direction	Lazar Dimitrijevic
Art Direction	Miroljub Matovic
Design	Lazar Dimitrijevic

—

The goldfish mascot was created in order to show the activities that help young people to start their own businesses at the Business Start-Up Center of Kragujevac. The goldfish rewards those who are skilled enough, inviting young people to compete for the best business plans and offer them training to acquire new business skills. The mascots grow with these people, changing over time and dealing with various types of jobs. The campaign ran from 2008 to 2010, with a poster created for each year.

The Children's Stamps

—

Design   Christian Borstlap

—

Christian Borstlap designed a series of stamps in collaboration with a Dutch children welfare charity. The Children's Stamp is a charity focused on the promotion of children's education. Working with the Dutch postal service TNT Post, the organisation has previously commissioned stamp sets that have helped to fund projects that support vulnerable children—the last of which raised more than 9.5m Euros for educational projects.

Making mistakes is the best way to learn

Together you know more.

Together is b

Together you know more.

Proberen is altijd goed.

Als je goed kijkt zie je meer.

Als je het even niet meer weet, gebeuren er vaak mooie dingen.

Iets saais wordt soms heel mooi
als je het andersom bekijkt.

Samen is leuker.

Vergeet niet te dromen.

Datum aanvang verkoop: 3 november 2009 / Artikelnummer: 291560 / www.kinderpostzegels.nl

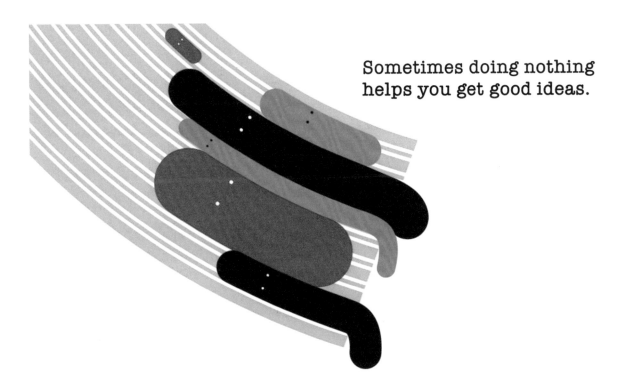

Sometimes doing nothing helps you get good ideas.

Adobe User Group XL

–

Studio   Momkai
Design   Martijn van Dam

–

The Adobe User Group is a community set up to provide
support for businesses and creative professionals of
all levels and professions in the Netherlands. Adobe
User Group XL is a conference that invites inspiring
creatives from around the world to share their stories.
Based on the "Celebrate Creativity" theme for the year,
Momkai created a visual identity based around a distinct
character, called "De Dasdrager'" (which roughly
translates to "The Scarf wearer") and is used on
promotional materials, digital projections, and signages.

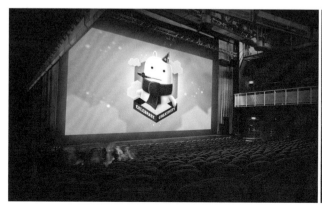

17 NOVEMBER
DE MEERVAART AMSTERDAM
CELEBRATE
CREATIVITY
ADOBE
-USER-
GROUP
XL/2010
Adobe
MEER INFO
ADOBEUSERGROUPXL.NL

Aqua Splash

—

Design	Melissa Rodríguez
Art Direction	Ana Estela Cantú, Cecilia Madrazo
Collaboration	Cecy & anne

—

Melissa Rodríguez was asked to conceptualize and design the identity for a water park. In response, a cute and child-oriented whale character was created to fit the theme as Aqua Splash is catered for children events.

Squiryl

–

Studio DHNN

–

DHNN designed the entire graphic communication
for the Squiryl Application, that includes original
illustrations, animation, mobile application user
interface, icons, interaction, website design and
development, games and much more! Squiryl
rewards you for going back to your favourite
businesses, collecting Acorns from every
purchase that can be used to redeem rewards.

Android

–

Design   Irina Blok

–

The initial objective was to develop a creative narrative and identity system for introducing Google Android platform to the market. As part of the campaign, Irina Blok created this little green dude and was meant to be an open source logo, very much similar in nature to the Android platform which is also open source. The logo was was released to the developer community without any brand guidelines. This helped to establish the identity for the new product and generated excitement among engineers. Initially, the logo was meant for the developer community, but it quickly became popular amongst the consumers, with millions of people creating their own versions of the logo every day.

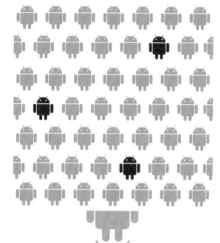

Suica's Penguin

–

Design   Chiharu Sakazaki

–

Suica is a prepaid card that contains e-money which can be used for transportation and shopping (whenever the IC card service mark is displayed) all over Japan. Since its launch in 2001, the penguin character designed by Chiharu Sakazaki has made a significant contribution to the widespread use and recognition of the card. The penguin was originally created in Sakazaki's illustration book, and was chosen as the character for Suica in an attempt to convey the convenience and user–friendliness of Suica to people of all ages.

Suica is a registered trademark of East Japan Railway Company.

Ippodo Tea

–

Studio   Bunpei Ginza
Design   Bunpei Yorifuji

–

As the shape of the teapot made by Ippodo Tea resembles a creature, the character was designed with the teapot as the head of Ippodo Tea's mascot. The mascot makes use of its head as a teapot, telling stories on the origins of tea and its traditions.

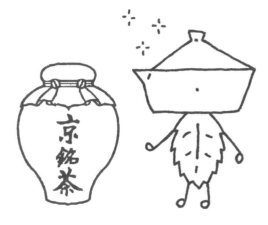

IPPODO TEA Co.

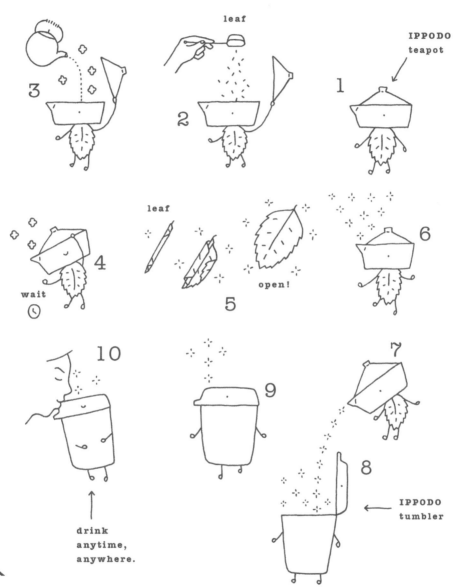

Retorna

–

Studio   Toormix

–

Toormix, a creative studio in Barcelona, was asked to design an identity for the project, Retorna, a deposit and return system for single-use containers, with characters designed to resemble the common bottles and containers that are discarded daily.

KLIMASKY

KLIMASKY

Hafslund Childrens Climate Festival

–

Studio	Commando Group design agency
Agency	Kitchen Advertising Agency

–

Held in conjunction with CC8 (Climate Conference 08), a top level climate conference in Norway. Commando Group design agency was appointed by Kitchen Advertising Agency to create a mascot to promote environmental engagement for young children.

KLIMASKY

KLIMASKY

Ameba

–

Studio	Blood Tube Inc.
Design	Atsushi Kaneko, Yasuko Kaneko

–

"Ameba" is the communication logo of CyberAgent, the internet service company. Blood Tube Inc. have created the logo with the hope that it will grow and expand CyberAgent, much like how amebas are constantly growing and changing rapidly.

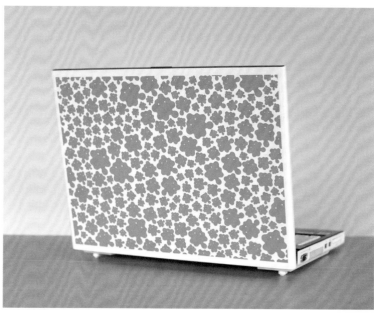

As hungry as
BEAR

Yoomoo

–

Studio   Bulletproof

–

The initial project was to create the brand positioning and visual identity system for a new frozen yoghurt brand. The goal was to establish yoomoo as UK's premium FroYo (Frozen Yogurt) category leader by creating a "famooly" of moos with distinct style and personality. Following Bulletproof's successful creation of the yoomoo brand identity, the agency was subsequently awarded the take-home packaging design project when yoomoo decided to enter the FroYo retail category in 2012.

chocolatetwistmoo

messymoo

nutritionistmoo

yoobake

fashionistamoo

angelmoo

devil moo

yoosmoothie

kickstartmoo

magnificentmoo

yoomunch

yoocrew

yooparfait

yoobrew

yoo'vebeenspotted

berrytwistmoo

sharingmoo

babymoo

with a pinch of salt
by kyra

With a Pinch of Salt

–

Studio   A Beautiful Design
Design   Roy Poh

–

With the tagline "It's only a cafe, don't take it too seriously", With a Pinch of Salt is a casual cafe that caters to students. The character, Kyra, is a "chef" that comes from a family of chefs and have been winning multiple culinary awards and appearing on countless TV shows.

Snack Lunch

–

Design   Claudia Martínez Ruiz
Photography   Claudia Martínez Ruiz

–

Claudia Martínez Ruiz is involved in the
creation of a new identity for a small fast food
business. Snack Lunch is represented by a
character and is located inside a university.

NATION: World Graphic Tour

—

Design   Cesc Grané

—

An illustration piece for the NATION World
Graphic Tour exhibition, in Rome, Italy. The show
requires participants to adhere to one condition—
to use the colours of the Italian flag to draw your
idea of Italy. As a pizza lover, Cesc Grané created
a fictional advertisement, with characters that
represents the ingredients, for an Italian pizzeria.

Mafia Style Pizzeria

—

Design   Dima Je

—

For the new pizzeria in Moscow, Dima Je developed elements based on the mafia and cooking theme, as well as created characters that will be applied across the collaterals, such as stationery, napkins, menus, packaging, etc. Each type of pizza is represented by a unique and funny character which will be used on the packaging. A colour palette of green, white and red—Italy's national colours—is used to reflect the origins of pizza.

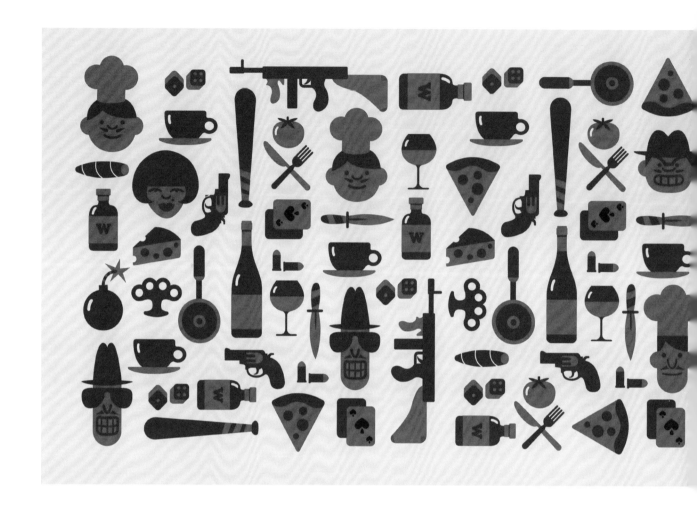

Monster Burger

–

Studio	BITE: design
Design	Rex Ng
Photography	Edward So

–

A branding project for a burger shop, BITE: design
designed a monster character as a mascot.
To position it apart from the rest, tailored
fonts are used in addition to the mascot.

Vypálené Koťátko

—

Design   Štěpánka Bláhovcová

—

Vypálené Koťátko is a cosy and nonsmoking café in Prague, where you can design your own cup while drinking fair-trade coffee or tea. The logo was designed after the name of the café, which is loosely translated as "Ceramic Kitten", as well as at the request of the client who wanted an image of a kitten in the logo.

Koultoura

–

Studio   FullFill

–

Koultoura is the pioneer of modern coffee shops in West Jakarta, and seeks to capture the market for people who yearn for good coffee as well as the casual coffee drinkers who are mostly residents of the nearby area.

The area where the coffee shop would be established is packed with students (high school and university students) and creating characters would be something that will appeal to them.

FullFill wanted the brand to be more approachable in terms of how the target market can relate these characters to their own personality: the gentleman (bear), the hipster artist (rabbit), the wise guy (owl), the cool musician (fox) and the stylish dreamer (penguin).

Kanpyo Udon

–

Studio   NOSIGNER
Photography   HATTA

–

Kanpyo Udon is a new udon product that uses gourd powder, and manufactured by The Oyama Chamber of Commerce and Industry in Tochigi Prefecture, Japan. Kanpyo are gourd strips that are commonly used for Japanese dishes such as sushi roll. NOSIGNER is responsible for creating a new brand that incorporates both the "Kanpyo" and the "Udon" noodle. The result was a friendly and memorable design, as well as being upmarket to compete with other traditional Udon brands. A new character was also designed to resemble a Kanpyo (gourd in Japanese), drawn in a way that resembles traditional Japanese calligraphy.

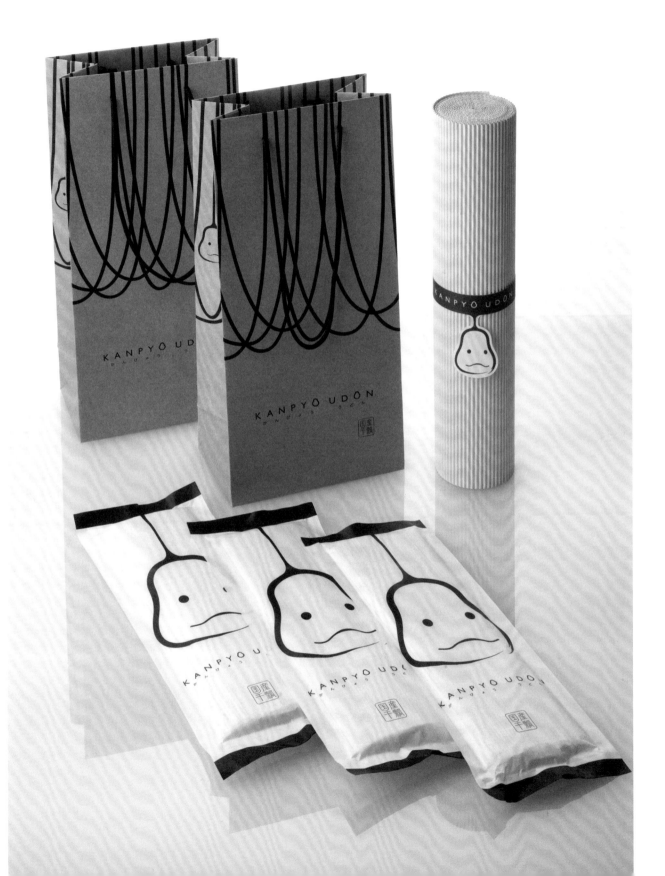

Lulu's

—

Studio	Stir LLC
Creative Direction	Brent Anderson
Copywriting	Brent Anderson
Design	Sarah Nelsen
Photography	Alistair Tutton

—

With more that 10 years in operation, the expansion of Lulu's Thai Noodle Shop sees an opportunity to evolve its brand through design. Stir has managed to retain its fun and modern Asian appeal while reinventing its colour palette into a fresher one. The vibrant colours selected were inspired by Thai food ingredients. Borrowing from traditional Thai imagery, icons and patterns were created to adorn booths, partitions and custom-made lamps. Outside, an illuminated signage draws attention from passers-by while a large wall facing the street has been converted into a billboard.

Hatched

—

Design   Sheryo

—

Hatched is Singapore's first egg-inspired all-day breakfast cafe. The brand identity is represented by seven characters, namely Olivier Omelette, Poached Pammy, Sweet Egg Ella, Boiled Betty, Scrambling Sam and Baked Billy—with each character depicting a different preparation style for eggs. The art direction draws influences from vintage comics that uses a warm color palette. The characters each have a story and come together to form the the menu.

FRYING FRED   BAKED BILLY   BOILING BETTY

SCRAMBLING SAM   POACHED PAMMY   SWEET EGG ELLA   OLIVIER OMELETTE

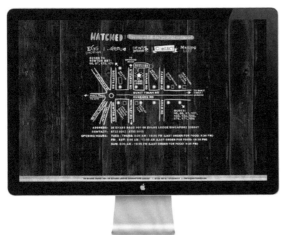

FRIENDS OF EGGS

BACON RAP 🅢 $12
A starter of tantalising Mozzarella cheese wrapped with tasty bacon served with fig jam dip, a great way to get the party started.

SAUSAGE PLATTER 🅢 $15
Enjoy three types of sausages (Chorizo, Garlic, and Tomato & Herb) all in one plate, served with homemade mash. Beer not included!

FRENCH ONION SANDWICH $14
A bready version of French onion soup, this sandwich comes with caramelised onions and Emmental cheese, topped with tender strips of steak on Ciabatta bread, served with homemade mash.

THE FULL MORTY $12
Go the whole nine yards with a Mortadella sandwich at its very best. Enjoy this dish paired with avocado, tomatoes, salsa and caramelised onions on Ciabatta bread, served with homemade mash.

THE MELT

VEGGIE : $8
Mushrooms, avocado, tomatoes and caramelised onions on half an English muffin topped with Monterey Jack cheese, served with homemade mash.

CORNED WAGYU BEEF : $14
Corned Wagyu beef on half an English muffin topped with Monterey Jack cheese, served with sautéed potatoes with caramelised onions.

HATCHLINGS
(FOR THOSE 12 AND BELOW, OR THE YOUNG AT HEART)

EGG-IN-A-WINDOW $4
The young ones play peek-a-boo with this simple creation of toast with a fried egg, yolk framed right in the middle, served with homemade mash.

PIPERADE $6
Scrambled eggs, colourful veggies, and diced ham all in one bowl of Spanish goodness, served with your choice of toast.

PBJ $3
Peanut butter + Jelly + Bread = Lots of fun for the kids, watch out for the sticky fingers...

FRENCH TOAST FINGERS $5
A stick-sized breakfast favourite for kids to enjoy one by one...

ANIMAL FARM $6
Let your kid's imagination run wild with delicious, fluffy pancakes in animal shapes stacked in one plate.

ALL STARTERS ARE MARKED WITH A 🅢.
1. $20 AND ABOVE FOR CREDIT CARD PAYMENTS. 2. NO SERVICE CHARGE.

BAKED, BOILED, FRIED, POACHED AND SCRAMBLED, WE HAVE THEM ALL & MORE...DISCOVER AND ENJOY THE AMAZING VERSATILITY OF EGGS AT HATCHED, WHERE YOU CAN HAVE BREAKFAST ALL DAY, YOUR WAY!

Osprey Brewing Company

–

Studio	justAjar Design Press
Design	Sara Alway-Rosenstock

–

justAjar Design Press was commissioned to design an identity for a private brewery located in Northwest Washington. The design was inspired by the totem poles and artwork of the Pacific Northwest Native Americans.

ChefBURGER

–

Studio   Tad Carpenter Creative
Design   Tad Carpenter, Design Ranch
Collaboration   Design Ranch

–

A collaboration between Tad Carpenter and Design Ranch has resulted in the design ChefBURGER's visual identity which expresses the build-your-own-burger concept of the outlet. To convey that there are no set rules to making burgers, a monster head was designed with ever-changing details.

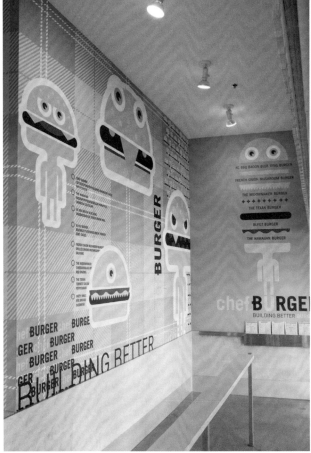

Nescafé Homecafé

–

Design   *Chiharu Sakazaki*

–

To increase brand loyalty, Nescafé Homecafé Winter Pack was sold with a special cup that has a marking for the right amount of hot water. With the cup, consumers can enjoy the best cup of Homecafé without having too much or too little hot water. Nescafé Homecafé Winter Pack comes in three flavours (Cappuccino, Café Latte, Choco Latte) and each has a unique cup that is illustrated by Chiharu Sakazaki.

NetEase 163

—

Design   VBN Innovation & Design
Collaboration Venco, Lea, Hanson, Cary, Onion

—

NetEase 163 is a leading Internet technology company
in China, with a large number of young fashionable
people with an average age of 28. NetEase wants
employees to have a better dining environment
and invited VBN to transform their canteen. VBN
propose the concept of "happy dining experience" and
created the visual experience for the restaurant.

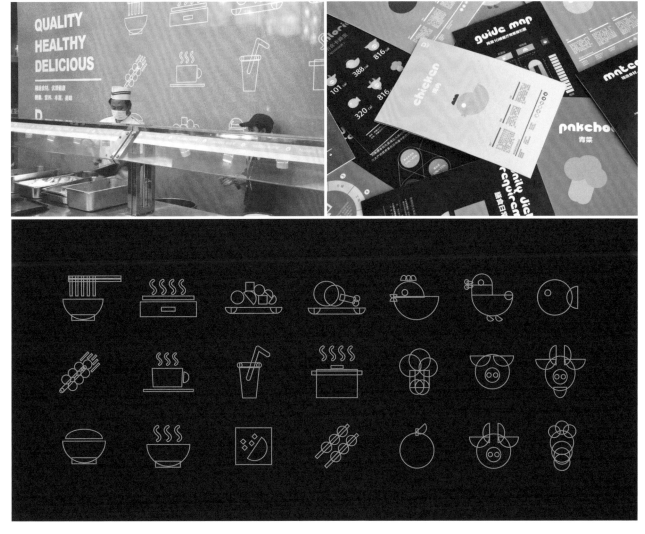

Wrigleys

—

Studio	Supervixen Studios
Design	Morten Rowley
Agency	DDB Sydney
Art Direction	Josh & John Baker
CG Animation	Fuel VFX

—

Wrigleys were looking to represent the lingering food taste that gums can cure by creating a series of commercials featuring cute characters. These characters "linger" around until they are scared off by chewing their product. The characters had to be cute, originate from food objects and be able to interact with the real world. Created in the style of "vinyl" toys, Morten Rowley of Supervixen developed over 100 characters with the directors before deciding on the final eight designs, which are further developed into commercials around the world.

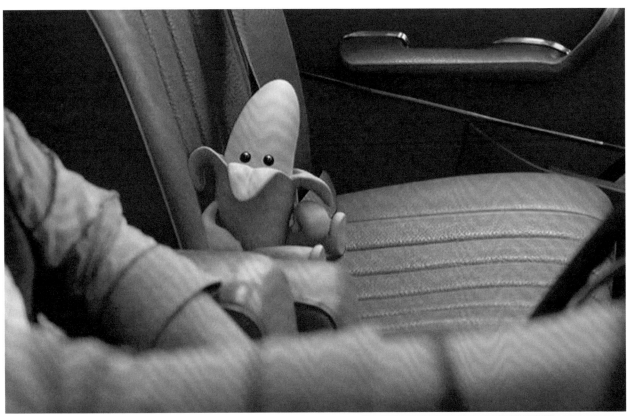

Tohato mobi

—

Studio   DESIGN BASE, Dentsu
Design   Tamio Abe, Hiroshi Deshimaru
©Tamio Abe / butterfly·stroke inc. All Rights Reserved.

—

With the launch of the new mobile-concept biscuits, characters were created to represent each flavour on the packaging. As a result, a variety of fun products were produced, with small but impactful packaging and advertisements that influences purchases.

Honeymoon Dessert

–

Studio   Tommy Li Design Workshop Limited

–

Honeymoon Dessert established its first home-style shop in Sai Kung in 1995. At the beginning, Tommy only added a nostalgic feeling in the brand image. Until recently, he created the "Sweet Monster" and kept innovating in order to enrich its uniqueness and to add value to the brand. "Honeymoon Dessert" successfully created problems for its rivals and gained considerable influence within the Food & Beverage industry. It has expanded into the China market and other Asian countries, and have since opened over 100 shops.

Kappa Noodle

—

Design   Mitsuru Ito

—

The character, "Kappa Noodle", was created based on the worldwide love and respect towards the Japanese instant noodles. Using a play of words, the word "cup" in cup noodles sounds similar to "kappa"—where Kappas are legendary creatures, a type of water sprite in Japanese folklore. These *kappas* are depicted with the instant noodles throughout the branding.

  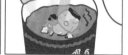

① Opening the lid.
① 蓋を開けます。

② There is a dry noodles and kappa.
② 干涸びたカッパと麺があります。

③ Pour the boiling water into the cup.
③ 熱湯を注ぎます。

④ Close the lid, Please wait 5 minutes.
④ 蓋を閉め、5分待ちます。

⑤ Will tell kappa, a ready to eat.
⑤ 食べ頃をカッパが教えてくれます。

⑥ Let's eat Kappa Noodle.
⑥ 出来上がりです。
　さあ、食べましょう。

ピザみたいな味
Tastes like Pizza

スンドゥブのような味
Tastes like Sundubu

脂っぽい味
Tastes like curry

たぶん醤油味
Maybe soy sauce taste

磯のニオイ味
Smell of the seashore taste

カレーのような味
Tastes like curry

しょっぱい人生の味
Miserable life taste

Tohato Harvest

–

| Studio | DESIGN BASE, Dentsu |
| Design | Tamio Abe, Hiroshi Deshimaru |

–

This project involves the renewal of the packaging design. Using the image of the biscuit—an iconic image through the generations—a smile was added to express the deliciousness of the biscuit.

Sabadì

–

Studio Happycentro
Illustration Andrea Donà, Andrea Manzati

–

Cioccolato di Modica, the first of many Sabadì's
products, adopts a typical sicilian way of making
chocolate made from Ecuadorian cocoa with six
different combinations. Sabadì sounds similar to
Saturday in Italian and is also the sixth day of the
week, and subsequently was used as the concept
when designing the six characters, six packages and
the crowner. Mixing inspirations from the glorious
Italian advertising age in the 50s to 60s, the usage
of type and design of the characters is clean and
timeless when combined with hilarious copywriting.

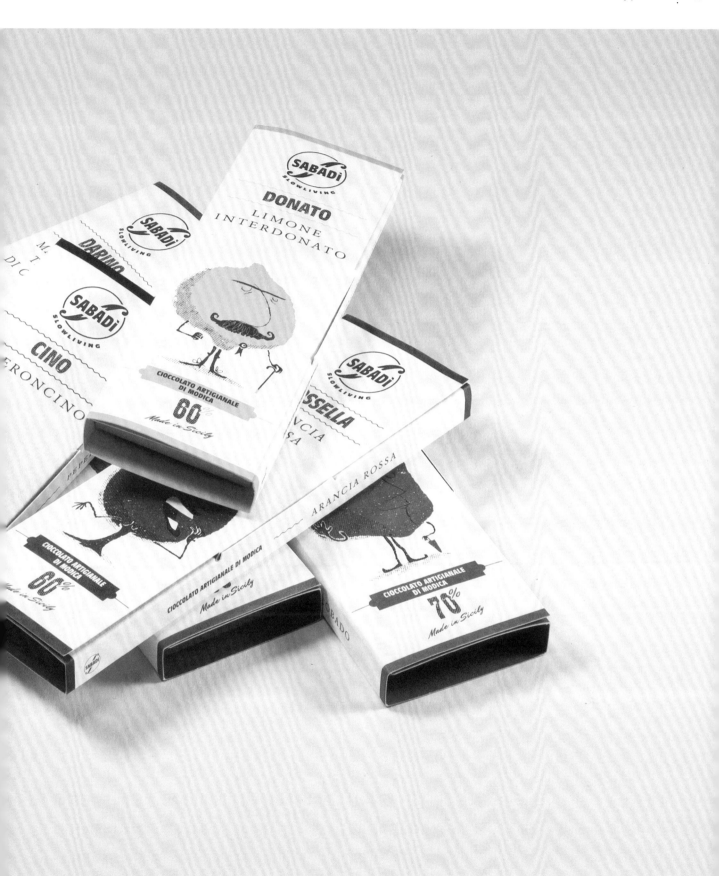

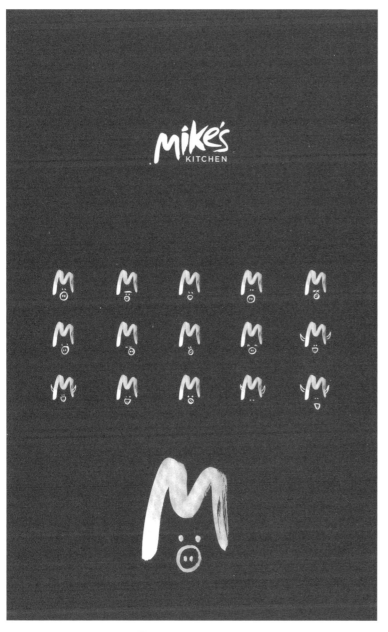

Mike's Kitchen

–

Design   Lucas Melbourne

–

Mike's Kitchen is a chain of restaurants in South Africa, and are famous for its succulent rib dishes. When Mike's Kitchen plans to expand their business by franchising the brand in Sydney and Brisbane, Lucas Melbourne was asked to refresh the brand for it's flagship Gold Coast restaurant that first open in 1996. Loyal customers do not like anything too fancy and the business thrives on providing the best and biggest ribs on the Gold Coast. With that in mind, "Mike" was created as a personal and straightforward response that will be used as a masterbrand to endorse future products and services.

Oichica

–

Studio   Canaria
Design   Yuji Tokuda

–

Located in the basement of PARCO Fukuoka,
Oichica is a boisterous buffet restaurant serving
delicacies that promotes local produce. The clanking
sounds that the walking dish character will make,
reflects the vibrant atmosphere of the restaurant,
with staff calling out orders enthusiastically
and happy customers laughing away.

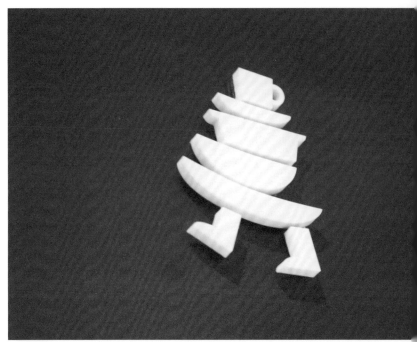

Little Chef

–

Studio	Venturethree
Creative Direction	Stuart Watson
Design	Mark Williams

–

To refresh the brand and attract a new generation of customers, Venturethree was asked to create a new branding for Little Chef. Venturethree created a series of "Wonderfully British" ideas to enhance the brand, like the iconic signage project where giant models of Little Chef and eating-out-British icons (lollipop, ketchup bottle, mug of tea, etc) were built. Along with the new brand identity, an internal and external signage system, a series of new menus, and the packaging for the new Good to Go range were developed.

To respect its heritage, Charlie, Little Chef's mascot, was kept but updated to be friendlier, more refined, with new energy and purpose, but recognisable. The colour red was kept, in addition to a fresh new colour palette of mushy pea green, raspberry ripple pink, English mustard yellow and baked bean orange.

SORRY
SACHETS
we only use Heinz bottles

Please tear here. Please tear here again. No, get a proper grip OK, try using your teeth. That's it, give it a bite, then try again with your fingers. Not too hard! Oh now look what you've done. Don't worry it'll wash off. It was mustard you wanted wasn't it?

Little Chef

As happy as

CLOWN

Paul Smith

–

Design   Tarout
Client   Paul Smith

–

Tarout created the characters for "Paul Smith × tarout: BUNNY PAUL" exhibition at Paul Smith Space Gallery, the only gallery space inside Paul Smith Boutiques, in Tokyo from 2011 to 2012. The story is inspired from one of Paul Smith's history, when he saw a rabbit from the window of a train to London for his first fashion show. The characters tell the story of how Paul Smith thought that having a rabbit would make the show successful, which failed and influenced what happened thereafter.

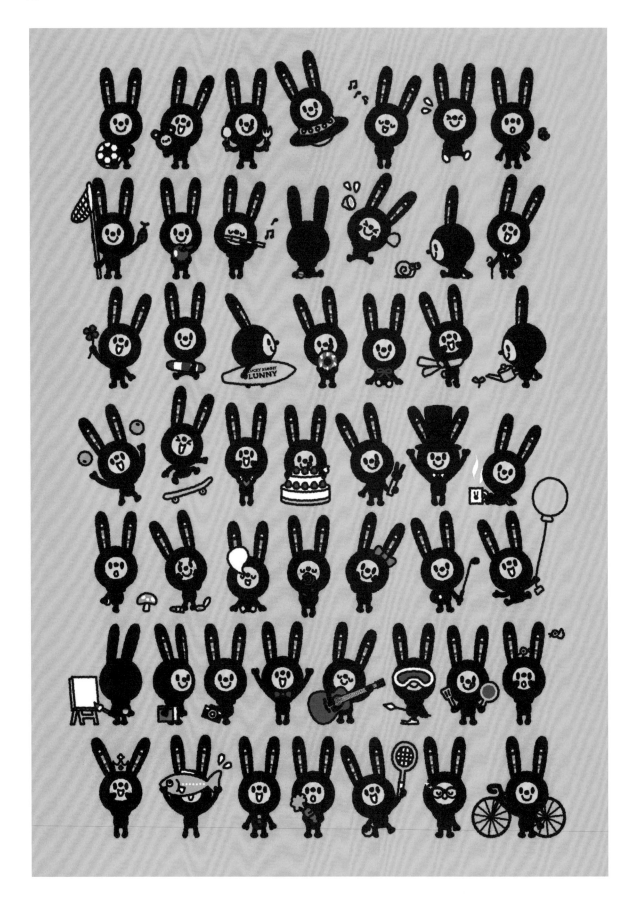

Bot Water

–

Studio	TDA_Boulder
Creative Direction	Thomas Dooley, Jonathan Schoenberg
Design	Brizida Ahrnsbrak

–

Bot Water is an all natural, low-calorie beverage, enhanced with vitamins, electrolytes and antioxidants. While these characteristics may not appeal to children, they certainly appeal to parents looking to give their children something healthy to drink. The goal of this project was to develop an identity and packaging design that makes Bot Water as appealing to kids as it is to their parents. The final product is a group of friendly and quirky characters, meant to inject youth into a brand with decidedly "grown-up" benefits.

Muncha Cruncha

–

Design   Lucas Melbourne

–

Muncha Cruncha is a start-up business that promotes local meal deals to help restaurants and customers. Lucas Melbourne was approached to transform a business idea into a tangible working brand and to strategically construct communication channels promoting special deals offered by venues as well as to reach out to potential clients. The response was a fresh, unique and friendly brand that is easily understood by everyone with the design of a mascot. Lucas Melbourne also designed a flexible system that could be tailored to suit different venues.

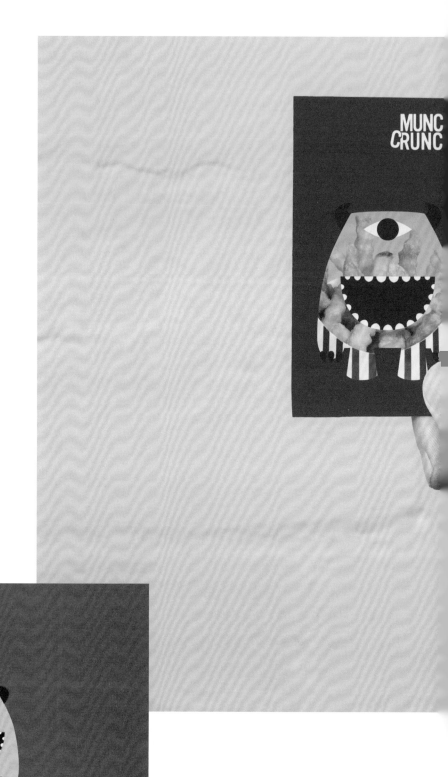

Hangame

–

Studio   DESIGN BASE, butterfly • stroke inc.
Design   Tamio Abe, Katsunori Aoki

–

An annual advertising campaign for hangame was
developed with the character "hanbird", which
was featured in in-house avatars and games as
well as promotional materials such as commercial
messages, posters and events. The comical
conversations between the parrot and the man,
reflect the fun one can have when playing hangame.

Mano Ravi

–

Design Trixie Chua

–

A revamp of a local Indian barber shop in the heartlands of Pasir Ris. The idea was to give the shop brand a modern twist that is friendly but at the same time retains the rough and tough vibes of a traditional Indian barber shop.

Sushitime

–

Studio	Creatifactory
Graphic Design	Gia Marescotti
Illustration	Gia Marescotti
Photography	Karen Leopold

–

Branding and identity design for Sushitime, a modern sushi shop that sells sushi rolls that everybody can enjoy on the go. The branding concept is based on the tagline "Just Roll With It". The illustration translates this concept while maintaining the youth and fun value. We intend to make the brand modern, youthful and with a touch of Japanese style.

Cacao Project

—

Studio   UrrutiMeoli estudio

—

UrrutiMeoli estudio designed the characters for
a teenage disco club. The characters are largely
vector-based and reflects teenage life.

ILoveChocolate

All
I ♥ Ch.   -2011#

IneedMonedita
I ♥ Tetra.

I Wish
You Were here

....

Cacao®
Colection

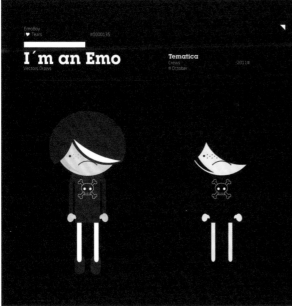

I´m an Emo

Vlad Dracul

All Musicicians
I ♥ Ch.   -2009#

Rockers 🤘
The Cacao Band.

Tematica
Bandas   -2011#

All Students
I ♥ Ch.   -2011#

Students
Vectors Draws.

Tematica
Escuela   -2009#

TheSeasons

Dic/Mar. #0000129	Mar/Jun #0000130	Jun/Sept. #0000131	Sept/Dic #0000132

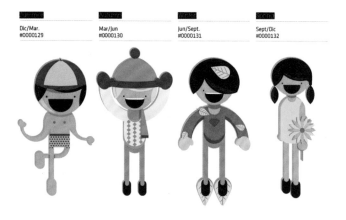

Enclosures
Vectors Draws.

Tematica
Libre   -2011#
00001234

Prizes Fever

–

Design   Cesc Grané

–

Prizes Fever is an advertising game powered by
e-commerce, with the website being inhabited by cute
characters and the mascot being a cute boy in disguise.
With the completion of each level, the mascot will
change his outfit until he achieve the status of God.

L25

–

Studio	DESIGN BASE
Design	Tamio Abe

–

The character "OL3" (read as O-L-San, where "san" means "three" in Japanese) was created for *L25*, which is the female version of *R25*, a free weekly magazine published by Recruit Holdings. OL3 also refers to the ladies working at offices. The characters, with unique hairstyles shaped like the characters O, L and 3, appears on the cover and contents of magazines and advertisements.

オーちゃん(23)　　エルン(25)　　ミーさん(31)

女子にやさしく、たまにきびしいマガジン

L25

RECRUIT
［エルニジュウゴ］

今週の推薦状
2008年上半期・マネーの基本もサラッと学べる
10万円が貯まっちゃう！
ごほうびカレンダー

ココロヲヒラコウ
「ヨガは"自分と対話する"時間」
SHIHO

社会
ひたむきな姿に思わず感動
女子でも
楽しめる **箱根駅伝**

恋愛
今年の出会いは成功？失敗？
2007年
総決算 **合コン事情**

その他もろもろ
寝化粧／カリスメン／鳥肌
タクシーの面白サービス
お腹の音／湯たんぽ／福袋

連載も絶好調！
自分のこと、どれくらい好き？♦男と女は…研究所
今週の彼氏♦チュートリアル／おもたせレシピ
20時からの週間TV番組表／波間の人魚占い

毎週木曜日発行!! **0**円
12/2007 **21**▶1/2008 **10**
こちらでもどうぞ▶ **L25.jp**

女子にやさしく、たまにきびしいマガジン

L25

RECRUIT
［エルニジュウゴ］

今週の推薦状
思いっきり泣く・笑う・怒る！
アグレッシBOOKで
感情デトックス！

ココロヲヒラコウ
「すれ違いこそ、素の自分を知る」
内田有紀

ファッション
スタンダードから最新流行のものまで
"**靴**" の種類を
総ざらい！

結婚
結婚シーズン…感動の嵐？、ドン引き？
最高＆
最低の **結婚式**

その他もろもろ
枕外来／洗濯ソムリエ
毎日エンジョイカレンダー
方向音痴／ケフィア

連載も絶好調！
ブランドって、どんだけ好きなのかなぁ？♦男と女は…研究所
今週の彼氏♦CHEMISTRY／おもたせレシピ
20時からの週間TV番組表／波間の人魚占い

毎週木曜日発行!! **0**
10/2007 **19**▶10/2007 **25**
こちらでもどうぞ▶ **L25.jp**

女子にやさしく、たまにきびしいマガジン

L25

RECRUIT
［エルニジュウゴ］

アンケートに答えて
「大根ロングビーチ入場券」を
50組100名様に
プレゼント！

今週の推薦状
時間に追われずのんびりと…が意外とむずかしい
ユルくて贅沢な
気まま旅の極意

ココロヲヒラコウ
「旅で脳内の空気を入れ替える」
田中麗奈

雑学
8月8日は「プチプチ」の日
プチプチ をつぶしたく
なる理由は？

生活
何日間とれる？ どう過ごす？
L25
世代の **夏休み事情**

その他もろもろ
ブランドビジネス／賞味期限
若年性更年期障害／デコメ
ラジオ体操／キャラメリエ

連載も絶好調！
恋人の恋愛経験って、気になる？♦男と女は…研究所
今週の彼氏♦坂口憲二／波間の人魚占い
20時からの週間TV番組表／サイテー男／アウトドア

毎週木曜日発行!! **0**
7/2007 **27**▶8/2007 **02**
こちらでもどうぞ▶ **L25.jp**

スタイルが光る女子のライトテイスト

L25

Coca-Cola
［エルニジュウゴ］

ボトルも
キラリ！ スタイリッシュなデザインがオシャレゴコロをくすぐる。
シンプル＆スマート
銀色のコークが新登場

カラダも
スラリ！ スタイリッシュなボディだって、もちろん大事。
オイシー＆ウレシー
ノーカロリーでいつもハッピー

ココロも
スッキリ！ スタイリッシュな気分で行こうよ！
爽やか＆心地イイ
ライトテイストでリフレッシュ！

スタイリッシュ
〈コラボ特集〉
輝く女性たち10人の本音をキャッチ！
彼女たちが
キラキラしてる
理由とは？
♦その答えは巻内特集で！

自分らしく、オンナらしく
飲んで
リフレッシュ！ ♦ もっと
スタイリッシュ！
こちらでもどうぞ▶ http://cocacola.jp

Chinese Wrigley Calendar

–

Design   Fil Dunsky
Agency   DDB Guangzhou

–

Fil Dunsky was commissioned to create character designs, illustrations as well as colour art direction for Wrigley's Chinese calendar. Featuring well-known heroes from different tales played by Wrigley product brands, the illustrations created are an impressive collage of vivid characters, colors, and high-resolution details.

Rivella

—

Studio   Loulou & Tummie

—

A family of over 200 character illustrations for the new Rivella campaign, Kicks & Thrills. The characters are featured in the mini games on the Rivella homepage, each having a unique simple animation & model sheet.

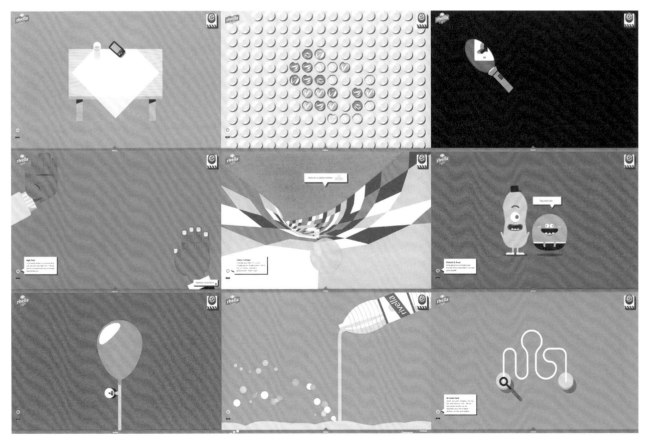

Frets

–

Studio   MEMOMA

–

Due to open in Mexico, Frets is a new fast food franchise that is entirely dedicated to french fries in different varieties and with unlimited toppings. For this project, MEMOMA used fresh and simple graphic elements together with characters to create patterns. These patterns are then integrated into Frets collaterals, such as envelopes, napkins, menus, gifts, etc.

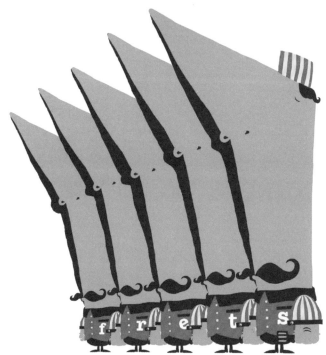

PO Kun Family

—

Studio   Frame Graphics
Design   Hideyuki Tanaka

—

PO Kun Family are mascot characters designed for the Joetsu Kokusai Ski Resort in Japan. After the launch, people loved the characters, especially when it appears on souvenirs or when developed into a character suit.

www.oRo.co.jp

ORO

–

Studio   Blood Tube Inc.
Design   Atsushi Kaneko, Yasuko Kaneko

–

"ORO" is the logo of a company that provides business
solutions and communication design. Blood Tube Inc.
created the logo which has a humorous and friendly
face by using the alphabet of the company name, "ORO".

Cubbish

–

Design   Winner Yang

–

Cubbish is based upon the story where an unemployed salesman takes in lost animals and subsequently builds a zoo for them. There are no rules, laws and cages within the zoo, as the zookeeper is good tempered and the animals will not leave the zoo. Cubbish embodies the idea that dreams will never be completed or achieved with rules and laws. Since 2006, Cubbish has become famous with its creative brand works. Winner Yang, the founder, draws his colleagues, bosses and clients as animals and gives each a specific and unique personality that pleases the audiences.

Fuji Chuo Kindergarten

–

Studio	10 inc
Design	Masahiro Kakinokihara

–

Fuji Chuo Kindergarten is a kindergarten at the foot of Mount Fuji, Japan. The logo symbolizes "the freedom of inspiration", highlighting the ideals of pre-school education envisioned by the president of the kindergarten. Reflecting this vision, the logo was designed to allow different interpretations of what it represents, it could resemble the ears of a bear, or turn out to be the eyes of a frog. The logo was also designed to create a cycle of joy, children dressed in uniforms with the logo will make their parents smile, and their parents' smile will bring about joy to the children as well.

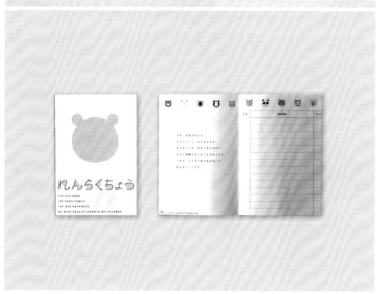

卒園証書

秋元　和歌子

平成六年五月十七日生

学校教育法による
幼稚園の過程を修了
したことを証します

平成十三年三月十七日

学校法人眞與樹小林学園
富士中央幼稚園
園長　小林直樹

第一七五号

Adams & Harlow

—

Studio	Christian Eager, Darren Barber
Design	Designers Anonymous

—

Adams & Harlow is a new British brand started by sisters Mary & Lizzi Adams, who are from a family with a long history in pork pie making. Their grandfathers were founders of rival businesses in Lincolnshire in the early 1900s. The Adams & Harlow brand identity captures the authentic family heritage whilst being stylish and with personality, featuring illustrations of both Mr Adams & Mr Harlow based on photographic reference. Across the brand they continue their long-standing friendly rivalry, both attempting to out-do each other with their "extraordinary pork pies". Mr Adams is wearing a "Pork pie hat", which he was known for wearing.

Marunouchi Kentei

—

Design   Tetsuo Hirano

—

Marunouchi Kentei is produced by its area management association to promote Marunouchi area in Tokyo, Japan. It aims to promote various attractions of the area and make people feel more attached to the town.

第4回
丸の内検定
MARUNOUCHI - KENTEI
2011年7月10日(日)検定日

会場：丸ビルホール他 / 検定料：3,000円（税込）

申し込み受付期間：2011年4月4日（月）〜6月10日（金）

主催：大丸有エリアマネジメント協会　特別協力：三菱地所株式会社

検定及びガイドブック問い合わせ先 ― 大丸有エリアマネジメント協会 TEL：03-3287-5386（平日9:30〜17:30）

「第4回 丸の内検定」公式テキスト
丸の内検定ガイドブック　好評発売中

【収録内容】丸の内に関する100問と解説 / [定価]1,575円（税込）　大手町・丸の内・有楽町地区の書店で取り扱っております。　丸の内検定 MARUNOUCHI・KENTEI

Tesco

–

Studio	Taxi Studio
Creative Direction	Spencer Buck, Ryan Wills
Design	Karl Wills, Roger Whipp

–

Following declining sales, Taxi Studio was asked by Tesco to inject some fun into their cookie and doughnut packaging to standout on the shelf and generate more interest in the category at large.

Jinqiao Foods Brand

—

Studio WONLEEYONCO Brand Design Studio
Design Director Guozhu Yang

—

Jinqiao Foods is a food company located in Shangxi, China, that specializes in the production of steamed buns and Jin-styled Mooncakes. Its original brand image is traditional and serious. With the help of WONLEE YONCO BRAND DESIGN STUDIO, Jinqiao Foods rebrands itself, with the concept of "the smile is the bridge between hearts" with a "cute and positive image." After the new branding is launch, the product and branding received rave reviews.

Make Shake

–

Studio	A Beautiful Design
Design	Roy Poh

–

Make Shake is a kiosk that allows you to create your own milkshake concoctions from a variety of flavours and mix-in toppings. Customised stickers were created for the milk shake cups to promote this unique concept.

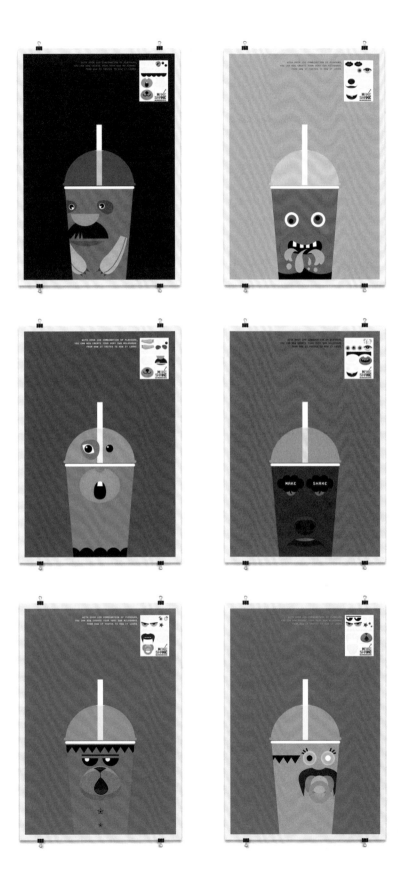

Family Mart

–

Studio	Ultra Graphics
Design	Rodney Alan Greenblat, Eiji Yamada

Based on the concept to make new products more lovable, Family Mart positioned these products as individual characters with its own name on packaging design, shop displays and as well as being featured in advertisements. Bagel-kun was the first character that appeared and with each new product, Rodney Alan Greenblat designed a unique character that make these products cuter and funnier, making them more lovable in the process. New characters are being launched together with the products every month with excellent sales record. For the 30th anniversary campaign in 2011, all the characters reappeared, 13 years after the original campaign was first launched.

KEN&MERRY

–

Studio   Frame Graphics
Design   Hideyuki Tanaka

–

KEN&MERRY are characters designed for Japanese fashion brand, SUPER LOVERS. A variety of clothes and goods were also created, each of them featuring the characters.

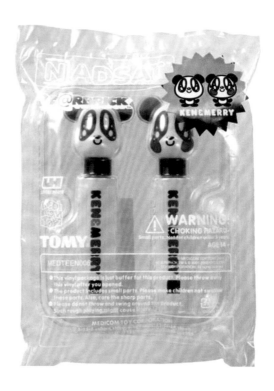

My Talker

–

Studio   Frame Graphics
Design   Hideyuki Tanaka

–

Designed as a character for an iPhone
application that reads out tweets in Twitter.

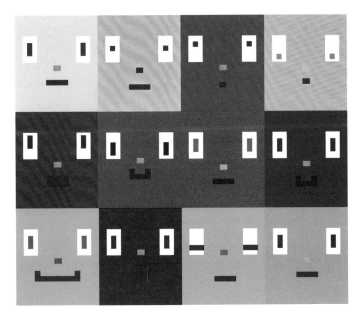

Sour Sally

—

Studio	Kinetic Singapore
Creative Direction	Pann Lim
Art Direction	Leng Soh, Pann Lim
Illustrations	Leng Soh
Writing	Michelle Lin
Accounts	Alicia Tan, Carolyn Teo

—

Yogurt is sour. Hence the name, Sour Sally. It became the name of the yogurt boutique and the unique character behind the whimsical make-believe world. She's not an everyday comic figure but a unique character with funny oddities. Entirely hand-drawn, right down to the tiniest detail. The character interacts with the environment and everything about the frozen yogurt boutique oozes Sour Sally.

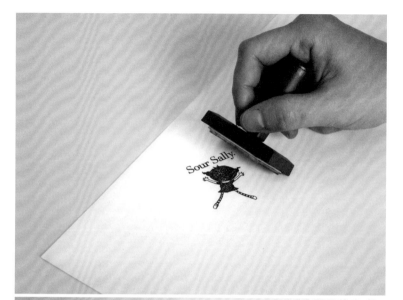

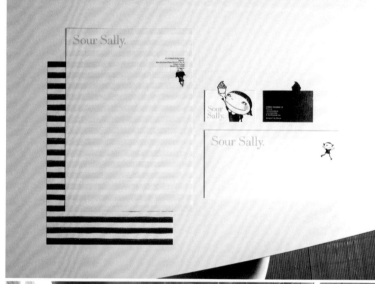

Ms Victoria Lau
25 Frankel Avenue
Singapore 458 215

Da Dolce

—

Studio   Tommy Li Design Workshop Limited

Loosely translating to "Sweetness" in Italian, Da Dolce was designed using the pistachio as its design concept by Tommy Li. A brand character, named "Da Dolce Kid" was also designed and was featured enjoying its journey through historical places in Italy such as the Vatican City and Venice. The brand concept is applied to all retail shops, staff uniforms as well as packaging.

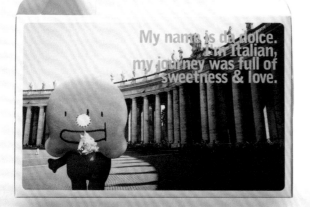

Lecca Lecca

–

Studio   DHNN

–

Lecca Lecca is a new kids couture clothing
company, and its playful and sweet identity is
inspired by Italian lollipops and sweet treats.

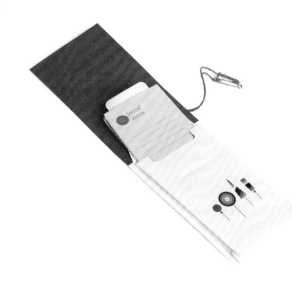

AGRI Design Contest 2007

–

Studio DESIGN BASE, butterfly • stroke inc.
Design Tamio Abe, Katsunori Aoki

–

Designed as the main visual for AGRI Design Contest
2007. Comical human-like characters and map symbols
were used to express the pleasure and design, as
well as to symbolise the future of agriculture.

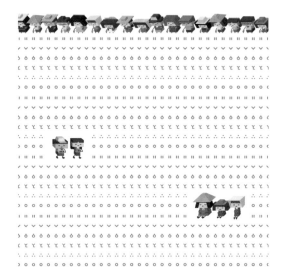

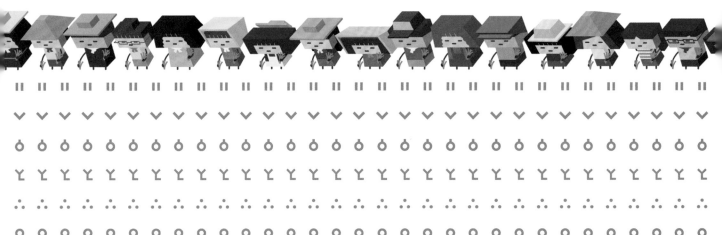

WAON

–

Studio   Draft
Design   Ryusuke Tanaka

–

WAON is an electronic money service launched in
April 2007 and is widely available across Japan.
The white dog with red collar was used as its
mascot in an effort to make people feel more
approachable and familiar with electronic money.
The character was named "Happy WAON", and is
featured on the original cards and goods, contributing
to the high visibility of WAON's branding.

arigatai.

おじいちゃん
むかしは船乗りだった
甘いものが好き
He used to be a sailor.
He likes sweets.

おかあさん
研究熱心
お料理などいろいろ挑戦
するが失敗も多い
She likes to take on projects,
such as cooking, but often
fails at them.

はなちゃん
宝物はクマのぬいぐるみ
負けずぎらい
Her stuffed bear is her treasure.
She is a sore loser.

ゆうくん
学校で好きなのは、もちろん給食
サッカーが得意だと思い込んでいる
Lunch is his favorite period at school.
He thinks he is good at soccer.

ハッピーワオン
お母さんと買い物に行くのと
歌をうたうのが大好き
He loves going shopping with his mother
and singing songs.

エリン
となりの家に住んでいる
ワオンのともだち
She is Waon's friend;
she lives in the house next door.

おとうさん
おかあさんの尻にしかれる
やさしいおとうさん
He is a henpecked,
kind husband.

おばあちゃん
昔話やこわいはなしを
するのがじょうず
水泳に通ってる
She is great at telling old and
scary stories. She swims regularly.

"Roman"

"wrap"

"a tumbler"

"Tissues"

Summer Social

–

Studio	The Hyspanic Gentleman
Design	Karl Cox
Collaboration	Sheffield Student Union

–

Following the success of last year's Summer Social end of term event, Sheffield University wanted to raise the bar with a more impactful approach. Using a bold colour system and imagery synonyms with the event and summer, Karl Cox styled the illustrations to be an explosion of fun.

Pepsi

–

Design   Hugo Silva

–

A entry created for a Pepsi competition,
Hugo Silva got the inspiration from
the shape of the Pepsi logo to create
a diversity of funny characters as an
alternative way to represent the brand.

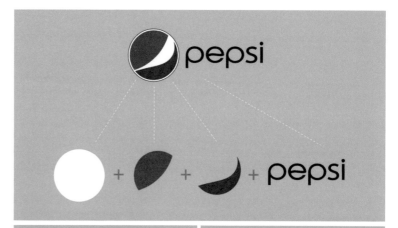

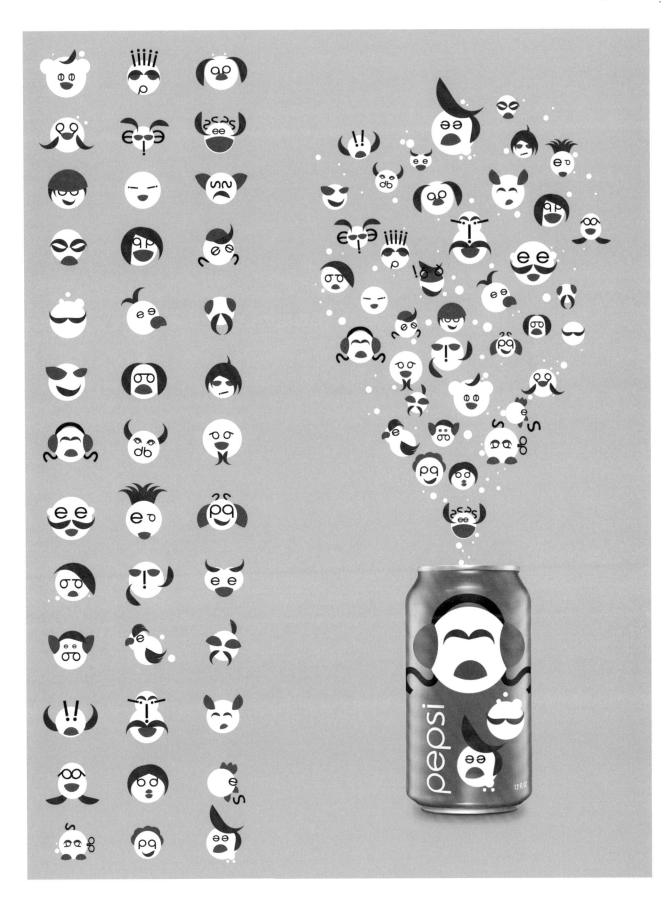

Yummo Yogurt + Smoothies

–

Studio   Tad Carpenter Creative
Design   Tad Carpenter

–

Yummo Yogurt + Smoothies is a dessert restaurant that offers any and every topping under the sun to go with its specialty yogurt and smoothies. It allows the consumer to create, build and weigh their own yogurt masterpiece and pay accordingly. This element of personalisation has been applied to the design of the restaurant's branding and identity, coupled with a friendly mascot and colour palette.

As Happy As Clown 249

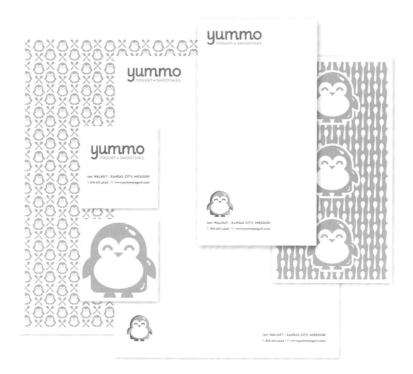

Expo Aanifeira

–

Studio	Atelier d'alves
Collaboration	Eurico Sá Fernandes

–

Project was developed for an exhibition for an organization called "Aanifeira". The concept was designed for children and young people.

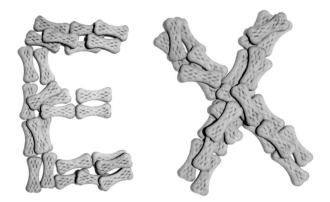

REC

—

Studio   Commando Group design agency

—

The characters, also called Rexies, are used for
internal communications in REC, a multinational
corporation developing systems for solar energy.
To communicate with employees in both Europe,
Asia and USA, the characters are made very
simple to make it recognisable. The cubical
form of the Rexies is similar to the REC icons
used for their external communications.

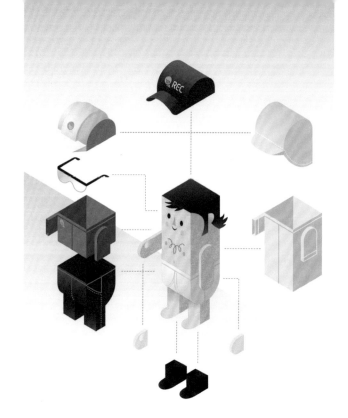

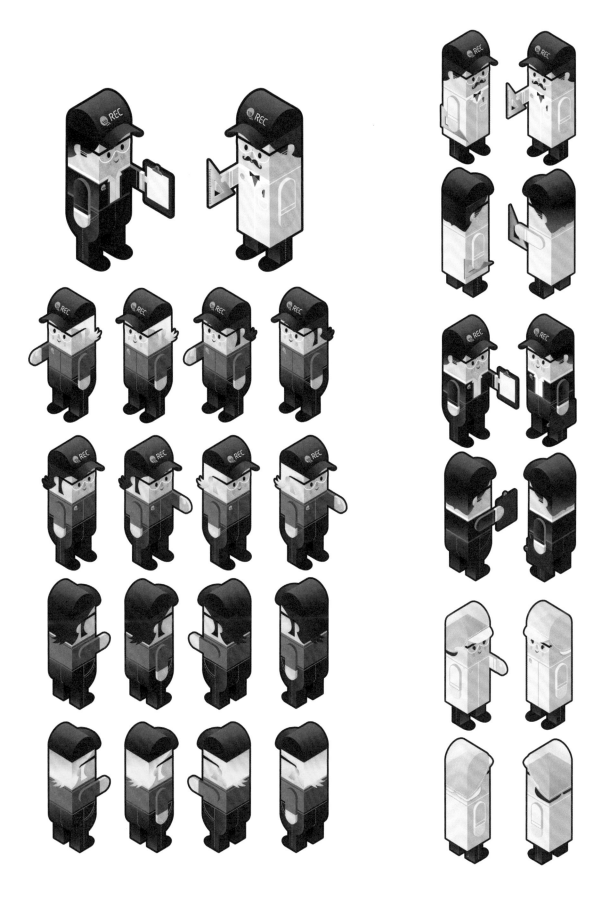

Pocarisket

–

Studio	MUZIKA
Design	Mizuki Totori

© Otsuka Pharmaceutical Co., Ltd.

This character was designed as the official mascot for sports drink POCARI SWEAT and is manufactured by Otsuka Pharmaceutical in 2009. The name was a combination of two words, "POCARI SWEAT" and "Sket". "Sket" or "Suketto" (助人), refers to the helper, making references to how POCARI SWEAT can support our tired bodies after an intense activity. Getting inspiration for the shape of the water droplets, the character is designed to convey a feeling friendliness and softness.

As brave as
LION

The Deli Garage

—

Design	Heiko Windisch
Art Direction	Reginald Wagner
Photography	Ulrike Kirmse

—

For The Deli Garage Kraftstoff Vodka flasks designs, Heiko Windisch creates four different designs, each depicting villagers, fishermen or a tribe trying to catch a monster. Each monster is an illustration that represents the flavour of the vodka inside the flask.

DETOUR 2010

–

Studio	BLOW
Design	Ken Lo, Crystal Cheung

–

Established in 2006, DETOUR is the annual flagship programme of Hong Kong Ambassadors of Design (HKAOD). In 2010, HKAOD selected the Victoria Prison to be its anchor venue, with the theme set to be "Not Guilty", based on the cultural and historical heritage of the venue.

A prisoner mascot was also created as a main visual and the colour scheme was inspired by the architecture. The supporting graphics and typography were mainly stencil-like due to its frequent use within the prison.

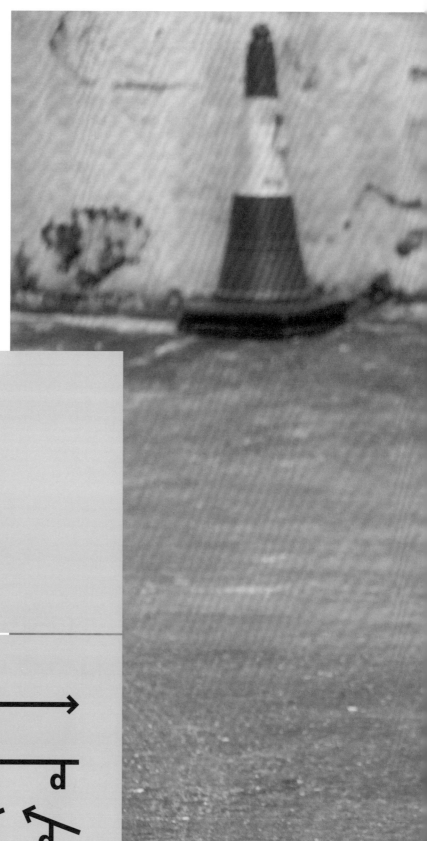

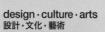

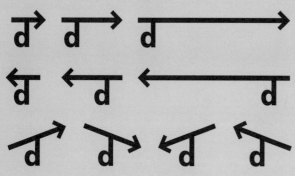

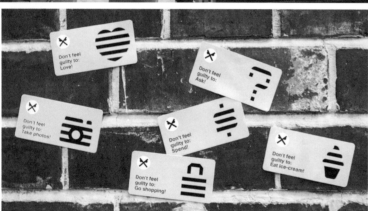

Job Hunting Club

–

Studio   THINGISDID & nekogato

–

Job Hunting Club is a pleasant card game designed
for dysgraphia students to learn about their future
pathways after school. The concept of this card game
is based on the Holland Occupational Themes (RIASEC)
which represents a set of personality types described
in a theory of careers and vocational choices.

We created the entire game starting with the
identity, including distinctive character design
of different careers, a set of colorful function
cards, and wooden game tokens that are all finally
packed as a tiny portable wooden boxset.

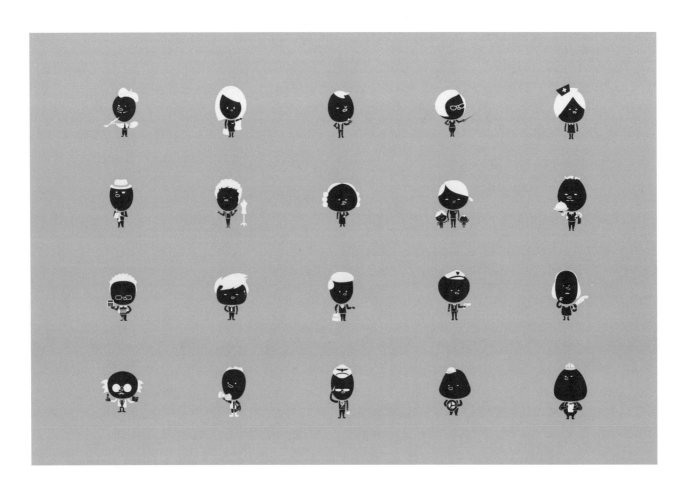

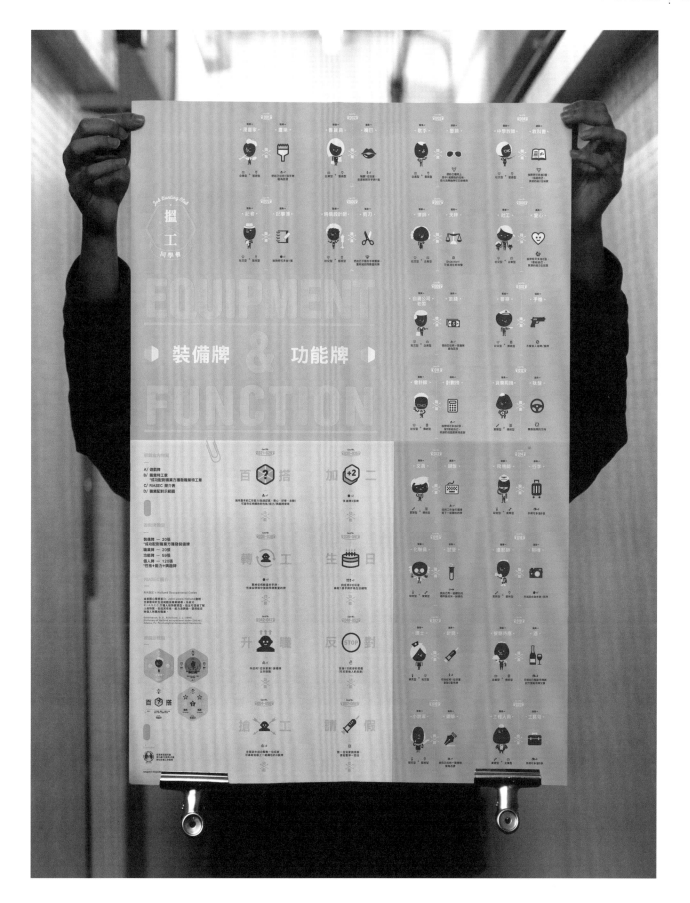

Spanish White Guerrilla

—

Design   Brosmind, Moruba
Photography   Moruba

—

Spanish White Guerrilla is a collection of "revolutionary"
wines created by Vintae. For the first time ever, the
nine grape varieties with the greatest international
prestige is being cultivated in La Rioja. Nine entertaining
warriors, inspired by the origin of the grape which
each represents, bring this unusual collection to life.

El Gamificator

—

Design   Cesc Grané

—

El Gamificator is a consulting firm that provides advice to professionals on implementing gamification strategies. The character which personifies El Gamificator is a Mexican Albert Einstein—a kind of crazy and tanned scientific who helps finding the best game for each website.

Travellama

–

Design   Hadar Geva
Guidance   Yirmi Pinkus

–

Travellama is Hadar Geva's final project
at the Shenkar School of Engineering
and Design, Illustration department.
The project is an illustrated brand
identity for a worldwide backpacker
information center, and includes the
design of the logo, brand character,
ten advertisements and giveaways
such as suitcase tags and postcards.

Strings for Kids

–

Studio   Touch Branding
Photography   Petra Hajská

–

Strings for Kids is a sub-event of the Strings of
Autumn international music festival where kids can
experience the diversity of music from different
cultures around the world. The personification of
music instruments symbolises various cultures and
nationalities with which the kids will come in contact.

Super Rebel

–

Studio	Het Echte Werk

–

A branding for Super Rebel, with the concept of it being a rebel, not just in name, but first and foremost in how we think and act. Super Rebel operate based on a belief, and that belief is that communication must rise above the ordinary to be successful. That starts with an idea that is incredibly strong and generates maximum attention for the brand.

Purple Dragon

–

Studio   Bulletproof
Illustration   Guy McKinley

–

Bulletproof was asked to help create a striking new brand identity and graphic suite (including environmental graphics and merchandise) for a new state-of-the-art children's members club in London, based around learning and fun. A range of cool children's characters were created by contemporary illustrator Guy McKinley to represent the different learning zones and age groups. These were featured on various applications around the club and on the web.

Mikos

—

Design   Thomas Bossée

—

Mike is a freelance developer, based in the UK, who commissioned Thomas Bossée to help him establish a fresh and unique brand identity. Mike wanted a logo which would represent three key values—trust, reliability and agility. Thomas Bossée was given carte blanche, and was allowed to be creative without stress or pressure. Built around Mike's initials, a logomark was designed. As the "M" stands for Mikos but at the same time for Mike, it seemed pretty obvious and logical to work with. Eventually both his initials ("M" & "C") were implemented in this logo, but with the "M" being the alpha element.

GHP Xair

—

Design   Taku Tashiro

—

The character was designed to promote the smart &
ultra high efficiency air pump conditioner by Osaka
Gas, Toho Gas and Tokyo Gas. The character was
subsequently developed to various PR collaterals such
as mascot suits, calendar, towel, strap, paper fans etc.

The Hang Gang

–

Studio	Analogue
Design	Tez Humphreys, Mike Johns, Barry Darnell
Photography	Mike Johns

–

The Hang Gang is a new store in UK, which stocks
toys, art, apparels and lifestyle products from around
the world, that are interesting and original. For
the branding, Analogue created a complete "gang"
of characters that enable the company to have a
unique and playful identity that evoles constantly.

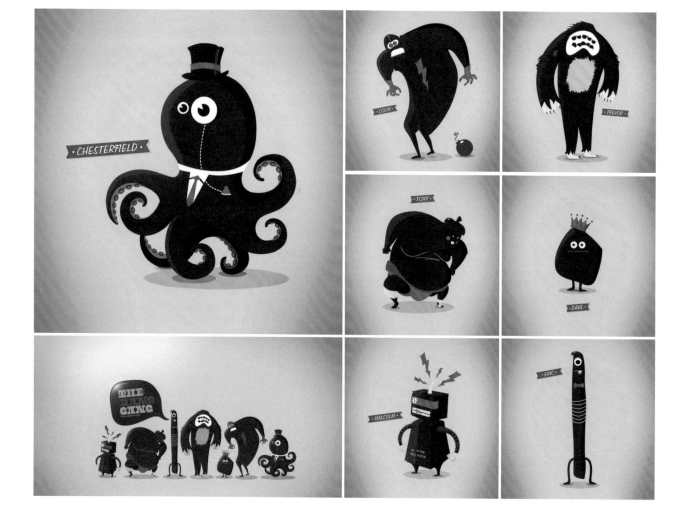

OH! SUPER MILK

–

Studio	Frame Graphics
Design	Hideyuki Tanaka

–

Character designed for the series of TV animation program and was subsequently further developed into various character goods.

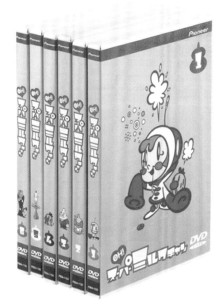
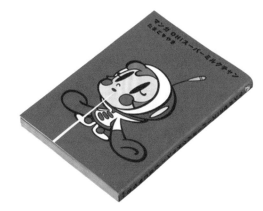

Alliance for Democracy

–

Studio	Peachbeach
Design	Lars Wunderlich, Attila Szamosi, Falk Hoger
Photography	Falk Hoger

–

Peachbeach created a advertisement on a tram to support the Alliance for Democracy, who wanted to send a message and say no to Nazis. The tram passes by the district of Oberschöneweide in Berlin, that have two neo-fascists hotspots—one is a bar, and the other is the headquarter of the Nationalists party. A whole bunch of heads were designed to show faces against fascism, advocating respect and diversity.

Don Belisario

—

Studio   Infinito

—

Don Belisario is a fun and whimsical identity for a new restaurant specialising in rotisserie chicken, a very popular familial meal in Perú. Rotisserie chicken, done in the Peruvian way, was first developed in a colonial-era hacienda (plantation), and hence the aesthetic during those times were used. To poke fun at the classic hacendados (the plantation bosses of the past), a whole family of them were created, but as chickens. Infinito rendered these illustrations in the style of vintage woodcuts to give them a sense of seriousness and respect. The intention was to come up with an identity that goes way beyond the logo and creates a platform for different interactions between the characters, constantly surprising and entertaining the restaurant's clients.

Brands with Character

Idea and Concept by

Curated, Edited and Designed by

working title & co.

First published and distributed by
Basheer Graphic Books
Blk 231, Bain Street #04-19, Bras Basah Complex, Singapore 180231
Tel: +65 6336 0810 | Fax: +65 6259 1608
enquiry@basheergraphic.com | www.basheergraphic.com

ISBN 978-981-07-9234-3

Printed and bound by
Shenzhen Hexie Printing Co., Ltd

Acknowledgements
We would like to thank all the designers and companies involved in the
compilation of this book. This project would not have been accomplished
without their significant contribution. We would also like to express
our gratitude to all the producers for their invaluable opinions and
assistance all this time. This book's successful completion also owes
a great deal to many professionals in the creative industry who have
provided precious insights and comments. Lastly to many others
whose names, though not credited, who have made a big impact on
our work, we thank you for your continuous support the whole time.

Future Publications
If you would like to contribute to our future publications, please email us at
hello@workingtitleandco.com